PARIS PORTRAITS

Walks in Gertrude Stein's Paris
by Mary Ellen Jordan Haight (Gibbs Smith, 1988)
is a companion to this volume.

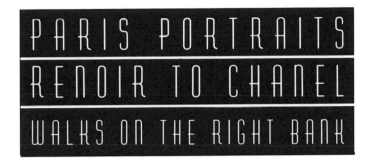

PARIS PORTRAITS
RENOIR TO CHANEL
WALKS ON THE RIGHT BANK

MARY ELLEN JORDAN HAIGHT

GIBBS·SMITH
PUBLISHER

PEREGRINE SMITH BOOKS

SALT LAKE CITY

First edition

95 94 93 92 91   6 5 4 3 2 1

Copyright © 1991 by Gibbs Smith, Publisher

This is a Peregrine Smith Book, published by
Gibbs Smith, Publisher
P.O. Box 667
Layton, Utah 84041

Design by Formaz

Cover photographs, clockwise from top left: Pablo Picasso,
Bibliothèque Nationale; *LeMoulin de la Galette* by Renoir, Cliché des
Musées Nationale; Oscar Wilde, Bibliothèque Nationale; Coco Chanel
by Man Ray, Courtesy Chanel, Paris; Charles Frederic Worth,
Bibliothèque Nationale

Library of Congress Cataloging-in Publication Data
Haight, Mary Ellen Jordan.
Paris portraits, Renoir to Chanel : walks on the Right Bank /
Mary Ellen Jordan Haight.
p. cm.
Includes bibliography and index.
ISBN 0-87905-361-5 (pbk)
1. Paris (France)--Intellectual life. 2. Artists--Homes and haunts--
France--Paris--Guide-books. 3. Celebrities--Homes and haunts--France-
-Paris--Guide-books. 4. Bohemianism--France--Paris--Anecdotes.
5. Walking--France--Paris--Guide-books.
I. Title.
DC715.H27 1991
914.4'361--dc20   90-14203
                                                     CIP

Tout passe, tout casse, tout lasse.

Everything passes, everything perishes, everything palls.
This book is dedicated to a courageous man, Robert M.
Almstead, and to the families of the other persons
with AIDS who died too young.

CONTENTS

THE PANORAMA

"To walk is to vegetate, to stroll is to live. Parisians stroll as they eat, and as they live, without thinking," according to Honoré de Balzac.

Paris Portraits is composed of eight two-hour scenic strolls through the Rive Droit (Right Bank) of Paris, with a focus on the arts from approximately 1850 to 1950 and their impact on western culture. The Greeks were the first to believe that the study and practice of the arts civilized a group of people and were a true exponent of history. By arts I include a broad definition of the creative arts such as visual, auditory, decorative, literary, and physical that includes painting, drawing, sculpture, architecture, music, drama, literature, fashion, and furnishings.

The strolls, or scenes, can be taken consecutively or individually. For example, if you cover Scene One in the morning and have lunch near the place Suzanne-Valadon, you can then begin Scene Two nearby. Through the literary scenes the stroller, or armchair traveler, will traverse the narrow lanes of the *butte* (hill) Montmartre and the raunchy flat areas of seedy bars and flesh shows, onto the Grands Boulevards to the theaters where the works of the innovative avant-garde musicians and playwrights were performed. Near the River Seine, the route passes former palaces of royalty and the elegant hotels visited by wealthy Americans, many of whom came to Paris to purchase expensive one-of-a-kind outfits from the *ateliers* (workshops) of the first *haute couturier*s (fashion designers). The stroller will then visit the fashionable rue du Faubourg Saint-Honoré, the renowned Champs Elysées, and the Arc de Triomphe, completing the artistic journey in the tree-shaded smart streets of residential Passy, an area not usually viewed by visitors to the city. The book of scenes is completed at the place du Trocadéro et du 11 Novembre overlooking the great symbol of modern Paris, the Tour Eiffel. With the glorious view of all of Paris and the special azure sky and fleecy clouds above it, this is the perfect spot to reflect and recall the words of actress Sarah Bernhardt: "Paris is a springboard I come back to to get a fresh *élan* [impetus or motivation]."

The Rive Gauche (Left Bank) is more familiar to Americans as the home and playground of the American expatriates than is the Right Bank site of power, tradition, and commerce. *Walks in Gertrude Stein's Paris* (Gibbs Smith, Publisher, 1988) described the ambiance of the *autre côté* (other bank) from 1900 to 1940. *Paris Portraits* concentrates on the art personalities and the settings in which they lived and worked on the Right Bank. Each address includes a word portrait or literary picture of a person or persons associated with the place. Gertrude Stein, describing her use of the word-portrait, noted: "I was making a continuous succession of the statement of what that person was until I had not many things but one thing." The rich environment that was Paris provided the background for artistic innovation and is the one thing developed from the many word-portraits in this book.

Around 1870 the stage was set for the modern revolution in the arts that largely took place in France, the new Babylon of Napoléon III and his architect, Baron Georges Haussmann. The impressionist artists and their literary counterparts, such as Emile Zola and the de Goncourt brothers, and composer Claude Debussy, reflected the society in which they lived, and their works recorded the daily lives of ordinary people involved in everyday activities. At this time quick visual impressions of the artist were depicted in luminous works that were often painted outdoors instead of totally in the artist's studio. French travelers to Asia contributed orientalism to music and the arts and crafts movements. From the International Exposition of 1889 to the outbreak of World War I, the Belle Epoque was the era of opulence, a period of luxurious grace. By 1925 the concept of harmonious integration had been recognized when the ballet gained new importance with its focus on collaboration between musicians, artists, writers, dancers, costume designers, and impresarios. Serge Diaghilev presented his Ballets Russes dancers in a production of *Antigone* (1923) written by Jean Cocteau, musical score by Arthur Honegger, sets by Pablo Picasso, and costumes by couturière Coco Chanel. Now symbolist art infused literature, art, music, dancing, and clothing. The *bourgeoisie* (middle class) attended performances of skits, songs, and dances at the bohemian cafés, cabarets, and music halls that were formerly the province of the working class.

The two personalities I chose to represent the excitement and creativity of this time period in Paris are Pierre-Auguste Renoir and Gabrielle "Coco" Chanel. Although they did not live in the city concurrently (Renoir had moved to Provence), their influence on western culture has endured. Renoir celebrated life and nature in his sensual portrayals of the Belle Epoque, while Chanel defined the art of dressing for the twentieth century.

Renoir lived from 1841 until 1919. His paintings of life in Paris represented the effect the city had on a visual artist and the artist's role in changing and developing the image of the city. When he left his studio to paint *en plein air* (outdoors), this latter nineteenth-century artist captured the city and its people as such vital organisms that the observer of the canvasses felt involved in the communal life. Renoir's vibrant impressionistic works treat the modern world as a joyful spectacle.

Mademoiselle Chanel, born in 1883, arrived in Paris from the countryside in 1909 as a twenty-six-year-old beauty already dressed according to her own simple style. Until her death in 1971, she continued to invent the look of the twentieth century, as well as its fragrances. Today her concept of elegance achieved by deceptive plainness and a maximum of freedom for the wearer have made her the most influential name in the world of fashion art.

Renoir and Chanel probably never met, but in 1939 she collaborated with his son Jean on his film *Le règle du jeu* (*The Rules of the Game*). The costumes designed by Chanel depicted perfectly the caustic image of château life in the thirties. When the movie was strongly criticized—it was even banned—Jean Renoir left France for good to become a director in Hollywood.

Looking back on the old Paris is like basking in the glow of the cultural revolution. It's easy to imagine life in the most civilized metropolis in the world because the results are part of all our lives and consciousness. As the English philosopher Herbert Spencer wrote, "Architecture, sculpture, painting, music, and poetry, may truly be called the efflorescence of civilized life."

Bon voyage.

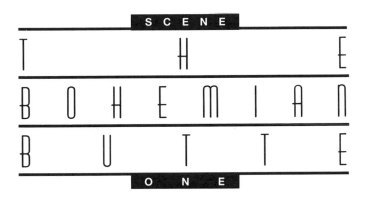

SCENE

THE BOHEMIAN BUTTE

ONE

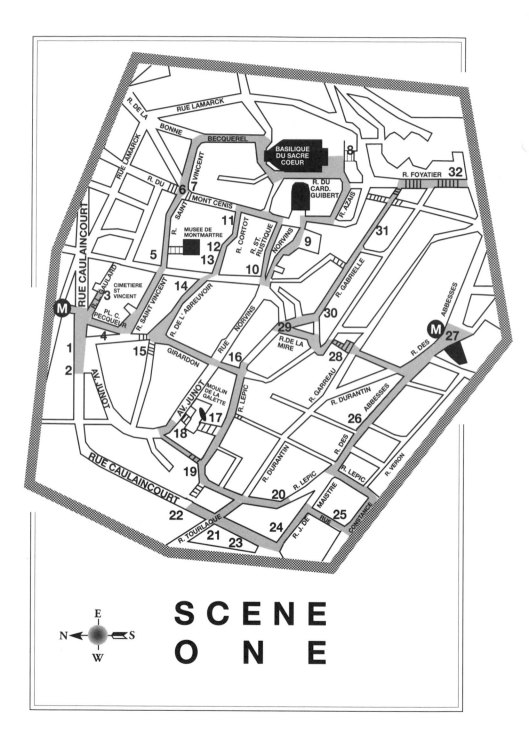

Montmartre, without artists
Futurists
Realists
Or Cubists
And without its many "jokers"
Practicing every kind of trade
Would be but a very dull place. (Anonymous)

Narrow winding dirt streets climbed to the highest reaches of the partly rural hill of Montmartre in the 1880s, when artists' studios dominated the scene. Windmills, vineyards, and family dairy farms provided the butte with a bucolic ambiance. Rents were very cheap and the artists were very poor. A walk around the base of the limestone hill today reveals remnants of caves that were former plaster of Paris quarries. Montmartre is the highest point in Paris and the mound is honeycombed with deeply excavated former mines.

From the latter half of the nineteenth century until the end of World War I, Montmartre was the traditional home of bohemians of all sorts—painters, poets, musicians, and models. By the twenties, the vineyards and family farms were subdivided, the lanes paved, and the slums redeveloped, which increased rents, driving the struggling artists and writers from Montmartre's glorious city view and that special light in the sky that still shines over the hill. Generally, the artists moved across the River Seine to the Left Bank neighborhood of Montparnasse. The Left Bank, made famous by scores of American expatriates, now became the center of innovation in art and literature in Paris and, perhaps, the world.

Métro Lamarck Caulaincourt
Bus 80
Upon exiting the Métro, turn around and climb the stairs to the street above, then turn right on rue Caulaincourt.

1. Residence of Charles Léandre
87, rue Caulaincourt
The twisting narrow streets lined with ramshackle sheds constructed from old planks of wood and junk hidden among tall weeds could be sinister dark places in the 1890s. Here lived the very poor—junk collectors, street merchants, and a few artists. According to Jean Renoir, son of artist Auguste Renoir, the area was "filled

with shacks inhabited by rag-pickers, and also less desirable characters." The shanties, built by the occupants, were free of sanitation and taxes. The rue Caulaincourt marked the bottom of le Maquis, the slum of wooden structures that was practically obliterated in 1895 by a catastrophic fire. Those left standing were demolished in 1900 by the extensive redevelopment program. The building in which caricaturist Léandre lived was part of the new construction. The cafés and cabarets in Montmartre published innovative newspapers in which political and social commentaries were illustrated by humorous drawings. From 1885 to 1900 satirical caricatures flowered; the symbols and images communicated the artist's inner thoughts and feelings about the important controversial issues of the day. Léandre and the early caricaturists were perhaps the first political cartoonists.

2. Studios of Pierre-Auguste Renoir and Théophile-Alexandre Steinlen
73, rue Caulaincourt

In 1910, at the age of sixty-nine, nine years before his death, Renoir worked here in what was probably his final Paris studio. Progressively crippled by gout, he then moved to the Provence town of Cagne where, seated in a wheelchair, his hands terribly misshapen by rheumatism, he continued to paint with a brush fashioned to his hand, which was as steady as that of a young man. His son Jean described his father's light brown eyes as having an expression of "irony and tenderness, of joking and sensuality, they always looked as though they were laughing, as though perceiving the ridiculous side first."

In the basement of this building, Steinlen, famous for his poster art and book and magazine illustrations, died in 1923. During his lifetime, few people, including the artists, took notice of his work depicting the desolate street life of the poor and the cabaret and theater life in Montmartre. In 1930 George Auriol, a fellow member of the community of Montmartre artists, published *Steinlen et la vie*, in which he wrote of Steinlen's achievements. This work, according to Armond Fields, "remains one of the best portrayals of the emotional milieu at the time these artists dominated the Parisian artistic scene."

After backtracking on rue Caulaincourt, turn right, up rue Lucien-Gaulard.

3. Cimetière Saint-Vincent

Two famous persons are buried among the interesting statuary in this small cemetery: Maurice Utrillo and Arthur Honegger. Appropriately, Utrillo lies here near the geometric houses and winding streets he painted. Look on the main path beside the outer wall for a marble headstone with a large cross and the figure of a woman.

Born in Montmartre on 29 December 1883, the great modern landscape artist Utrillo died on 6 December 1955 in the town of Dax. Utrillo was the son of painter Suzanne Valadon (whose lover was Henri de Toulouse-Lautrec) and Adrian Boissy, an insurance-clerk-turned-painter and a heavy drinker. Valadon decided that Boissy was not a worthy father to the moody, disturbed child and when the boy was eight she persuaded Spanish art historian and critic Miguel Utrillo y Mollins to adopt him so he would have the Utrillo family name. The new father never helped raise Maurice or support him financially. In 1935, when he was forty-eight years old, Utrillo married the widow Lucie Valore; she is buried nearby.

Before exiting the cemetery, turn back on the main road to the tomb of the Swiss composer Arthur Honegger (1892–1955), a member of the group of modern French composers known as The Six. His experimental musical style was heavily influenced by Richard Wagner and Johann Sebastian Bach. Besides composing jazz, Gregorian chants, tone poems, and operas, he composed for the Ballets Russes.

4. Place Constantin-Pecqueur

After exiting the cemetery, pause at the rear of the small park to see the fountain with a statue depicting a man and woman embracing; it is dedicated in memory of Steinlen. Now walk up rue Saint-Vincent one block to rue des Saules.

5. Le Lapin Agile café
4, rue des Saules

Directly across from the only vineyard left on Montmartre is the former Cabaret des Assassins, which, in 1880, was renamed for a sign designed by André Gill. The illustration depicted a rabbit wearing a red bow tie and jumping nimbly out of a copper cooking pot. Originally, the café was called Le Lapin à Gill (the rabbit by

5

Gill), but it became better known as Le Lapin Agile (the nimble rabbit). The former eighteenth-century coach inn was a favorite stop for Montmartre artists and writers such as Max Jacob, Guillaume Apollinaire, Picasso, Utrillo, and Paul Gauguin.

On wood tables lighted by lamps veiled in red silk scarves, Berthe, proprietor and entertainer Frédéric Gérard's wife, served a Burgundian dinner for two francs.

A well-told story details the raucous evening when writer Roland Dorgelès attached a paintbrush to the twitching tail of bushy-bearded Frédé's unhousebroken donkey "Lolo" and then submitted the "impressionistic" ass-painted canvas to the juryless Salon des Indépendants in 1910 under the title *Sunset on the Adriatic* by Boronali.* This result of Dorgelès's effort to mock the art establishment was sold for four francs, but history does not record the name of the buyer of the donkey's work of art.

A huge carved crucifix dominated one wall of the large salon, and in 1905 Frédé commissioned Picasso to create a decoration to hang next to the religious symbol. The result was *Au Lapin Agile* (At the Agile Rabbit), a rose-period piece in which Picasso portrayed himself as a harlequin and Frédé is pictured in the background. It was based on Toulouse-Lautrec's *Le divan japonais* (Scene Two, #4). According to Picasso, he painted it in exchange for free meals and drinks. Frédé sold the work (it had not been framed) in 1912 and it eventually landed in the extensive collection of the late American heiress Joan Payson Whitney. It was sold at auction in November 1989 for $40.7 million.

6. Rue Saint-Vincent and rue du Mont-Cenis

Lucien Pissarro, as well as Georges Seurat and Maximilien Luce, pictured this sunlit intersection in the winter of 1889–90. Although Pissarro's work illustrates the feeling of Montmartre as a small provincial town, a look at the view from this spot reveals the hill's split identity. It was separate from the cosmopolitan city sprawling below, but its residents depended upon the transportation services and merchants located at the base of the hill.

---

*From Aliboron, the foolish donkey immortalized by La Fontaine.

Pierre Prins, Le Cabaret du Lapin Agile á Montmartre.
(Musées de la Ville de Paris by SPADEM 198.)

7. Residence of Hector Berlioz
11 bis, rue Saint-Vincent

The plaque on the corner building denotes the residence of musician Hector Berlioz from 1834 to 1836 and the place where he composed *Harold in Italy* and *Benvenuto Cellini.* Although he is referred to by many musicologists as the greatest French musician of the nineteenth century, at the time of his death in 1869, Berlioz's music was unpopular, his writing sarcastic, his wit caustic, and his friends few. Concerned not only with music, but also politics, literature, and art, Berlioz, at about the same time as the romantic writers and artists, began experimenting with novel subjects and broke with formal musical tradition. This isolated him because at that time musicians, as a group, had less impact on society and culture than did Victor Hugo and his fellow writers or painters like Courbet and Delacroix. Berlioz died never knowing that he had laid the foundation of modern French music.

Continue up rue Saint-Vincent and turn right on rue de la Bonne Becquerel.

Le Basilique du Sacré-Coeur around 1910. (*From* Paris Illustrated, *courtesy of Thomas Gee.*)

8. Basilique du Sacré-Coeur

Like the white-sugar-frosted top of a wedding cake, Sacré-Coeur crowns the summit of the hill. Although construction on the church began in 1875, the first service was not held until 1891.

In his book *Black Spring* (1936), Henry Miller describes walking up the butte

> *and suddenly the street opens wide its jaws and there, like a still white dream, like a dream embedded in stone, the Sacré-Coeur rises up at late afternoon and the heavy whiteness of it is stifling. A heavy, somnolent whiteness, like the belly of a jaded woman. . . . It's in the night that Sacré-Coeur stands out in all its stinking loveliness. Then it is that the heavy whiteness of her skin and her humid stone breath clamps down on the blood like a valve.*

After walking around the church to see the incredible view of the city, walk a short block to the west.

9. Place du Tertre

Traditionally, the neighborhood artists displayed their works in the small park. Today, tour buses disgorge hordes of tourists seeking to recapture the bohemian ambiance of the late nineteenth century. Questionable artists paint faux Utrillos while bow-tied waiters scurry around to deliver what are almost French fast-food meals. The seedy area must have had a village feeling when American author John Dos Passos wrote: "I shall send my heart to be preserved in a *pichet* of *Vin de Beaujolais* in the restaurant in the place du Tertre on the summit of Montmartre." You might try eating at the restaurant La Bohème where the plaque states that Suzanne Valadon and her son Maurice Utrillo ate between 1919 and 1935.

Exit on rue Norvins and turn right at the first street.

10. Studio of Vincent van Gogh
18, rue Saint-Rustique

When van Gogh joined his brother, Theo, in Paris in 1886, he maintained a studio for painting large canvasses in this building. A year and a half later, while living in Provence, the artist wrote to Theo:

I think that all the talk of high prices paid for Millets, etc., lately has made the chances of merely getting back one's painting expenses even worse. It is enough to make you dizzy. So why think about it? It would only daze our minds. Better to seek a little friendship and to live from day to day.

Van Gogh sold only one work during his lifetime, yet in 1987 his oil depiction of irises brought $53.9 million dollars at auction. The $82.5 million paid for his portrait of Dr. Paul Gachet in 1990 is a record price for a painting sold at auction.

Continue to the corner and turn left.

11. Residence of Erik Satie
6, rue Cortot

For eight years, Satie lived here in a small studio where he composed fanfares for the mysterious opening ceremonies of the esoteric Rosicrucian Salons. The "closet" room was rigged up with a series of locks and transoms that allowed air and light to enter from the landing but kept out curious peeks of passersby. A piano was squeezed into the room along with a bed, a chest, and a bookshelf. In a painting by the Spanish Catalan artist Santiago Rusiñol, Satie is pictured sitting on a stool before the small fireplace.

After receiving an inheritance from his father, Satie purchased a dozen identical grey corduroy suits which he wore for "scores of years." Eccentric, even a little mad, his humor and behavior were often absurd. Breaking with the Rosicrucians, Satie founded his own religion: the Metropolitan Church of the Art of Jesus the Conductor. Two issues of the official publication of the church appeared, both written, published, and paid for by Satie. There is no record of church meetings.

In the first of his two separate musical careers, Satie worked as a second pianist in Rodolphe Salis's Chat Noir café and, wearing

Ramon Casas, The Bohemian. *Portrait of Erik Satie on Montmartre, 1891. (Northwestern University Library.)*

a flowing tie and a soft velvety felt béret, he grew a beard and adopted the demeanor of the bohemian cabaret musician. Playing the piano in various Montmartre cabarets did not stop Satie from serious composing, but the innovative style of his music during this period reflects the influence of the popular music-hall tunes he played and heard. The company of his painter friends—the Spanish modernists—also affected Satie's style, as his French biographer Templier states: "Through contact with them his sense of humor, his musical aesthetic, and his bohemian spirit took shape." In a lecture to his friend Debussy, Satie spoke of the development of musical style: "Why not make use of the means of representation which Claude Monet, Cézanne, and Toulouse-Lautrec were showing us?"

Without warning, in 1898 Satie moved his belongings in a wheelbarrow to a southern suburb of Paris. He appeared to need solitude and absence from the forced gaiety of life in Montmartre in order to devote his time to work and study.

12. Musée de Montmartre
12–14, rue Cortot

The museum is appropriately located in a seventeenth-century house that became home to many French artists. Walk through the museum shop to the enclosed garden, passing a studio on your left, and then to the house in the rear where, in his first home in Paris, Renoir enjoyed a glorious view of the city and country beyond. He paid only 1,000 francs ($200) yearly for the simply furnished dilapidated building. During 1875–76 he painted his famous depiction of the nearby Moulin de la Galette, daily carrying a large piece of canvas just a short distance. The well-known café scene was described by art historian John Rewald as "possibly the finest work Renoir painted" when the canvas was sold in 1990 for $78.1 million, an auction record for impressionist art.

Suzanne Valadon and Utrillo inhabited the house from 1906 to 1909, and she painted the garden as she viewed it from a second-floor window. Once an acrobat, Valadon's circus days ended with a fall from a trapeze and she became an artist's model, posing for many Montmartre artists, including Renoir and Degas. The latter encouraged her painting and was the first to purchase her work. At the age of twenty-eight she moved here, next to Satie's home, and in 1893 began a stormy love affair with him which led to her portrait of the handsome bearded and shaggy-haired bohemian. When their quarrels became especially wild, Satie defended his position through proclamations questioning the virtue of Valadon which he displayed from his window facing on the rue Cortot.

13. Residence of Maximilien Luce
16, rue Cortot

The neoimpressionist Luce employed the technique of divisionism, otherwise known as pointillism, in his highly colored realistic representations of given events. Small exact dots of paint were blended together with light to give the effect of color completely covering the canvas. Originally trained as a printmaker, he contributed illustrations to anarchist periodicals in the 1870s. His work titled *Une rue de Paris sous la Commune*, which hangs in the Musée d'Orsay, offers a retrospective view of the Commune of Paris in 1871 when more than 17,000 extreme leftist political supporters were executed by the Prussian-backed French government troops.

14. La Maison Rose
2, rue de l'Abreuvoir

I am Rose but I am not rosy
all alone but not very cosy
I am Rose and awhile I am Rose
Well well Rose is Rose.
(Gertrude Stein)

La Maison Rose, a favorite restaurant of artists like Utrillo and Picasso. (Mary Ellen Jordan Haight.)

The "pink house" café was a favorite of nearby residents Utrillo and Picasso. Utrillo created an oil picturing it almost as it appears today. You can imagine Picasso on a warm summer day sitting at one of the tables that still are placed on the sidewalk, enjoying the dazzling view of the city and waiting for his friend Gertrude Stein to pass by on her route to his studio. Not only is the building's exterior still pink, but so is the cutlery.

At the end of the street turn into the walkway.

15. Residence of Auguste Renoir (13), rue Girardon, Allée des Brouillards

What is now a beautiful garden was an orchard in 1895, when wild rose bushes lined the dirt path that ran alongside the deep rectangular building that faced on rue Girardon. The Renoir family lived in number 6 on the two upper floors with a small studio in the attic, from which Renoir observed the devastating fire which turned the wooden buildings of le Maquis into rubble. The difficulty of climbing the steep hill on winding dirt paths was largely compensated "by the low rents, the fresh air, the cows, the lilacs and the roses" wrote Jean Renoir.

Now turn left on rue Girardon.

16. Studio of Eugène Delâtre 87, rue Lepic

In his studio here printmaker Delâtre not only produced his own fine etchings but published the Imprimerie Artistique collection of etchings by other famous artists. From 1876 he collaborated with his father, Auguste Delâtre, whose studio on the Left Bank was destroyed during the Franco-Prussian War in 1871. Afterward the father spent time in England working with artists James Tissot and Jules Dalou, then returned to France to collaborate with his son.

17. Le Moulin de la Galette 79, rue Lepic

At the age of twenty-six, Renoir painted the monumental *Bal du Moulin de la Galette* (*The Dance Hall of the Moulin de la Galette*), and if you peer through the trees to the top of the hill you can still catch a glimpse of the old windmill. The gardens and buildings were a café, bar, and dance hall in 1898, when the entrance fee was twenty-five centimes for women and fifty for men. The Moulin did not attract the clientele of the cabarets and bals (dance halls) of the nightlife at the bottom of the butte, but the local workmen, housemaids, models, and artists liked its semirural ambiance and met their friends here. "Invasions by foreigners were very rare," wrote American art student W. C. Morrow.

Just beyond the windmill, turn through an iron gate, climb the stairs, and follow the path to another gate. Exit and turn right on avenue Junot to the first building on your right.

18. Home of Tristan Tzara
15, avenue Junot

The Rumanian poet Tzara, together with the artist Hans Arp, founded the dada art movement in Zurich, Switzerland. In 1920, they joined American painter Francis Picabia in Paris where, with artists André Masson and Antonin Artaud, they decreed that cubism was dead. By 1924 the group had joined with André Breton and the surrealists.

Two years later, in 1926, Tzara brought the Viennese architect Adolf Loos, whose modern designs Tzara considered dadaist in style, to Paris to design this five-story house. The square-cubed building is set against a hillside with a lounge and dining room on the third level and a terrace off the rear. The entry is on the second level above the ground. (Remember, in Europe the first floor is designated as the one above the ground floor.) The strange house reflects the eccentricism of its owner-builder.

When Gertrude Stein referred to Tzara as "like a pleasant and not very exciting cousin," he called her book *The Autobiography of Alice B. Toklas* "a considerable display of sordid anecdotes destined to make us believe that Miss Gertrude Stein is in reality a genius." Stein and Toklas were described by him as "two maiden ladies greedy for fame and publicity"!

Reverse your route back to rue Lepic.

19. Residence of George Auriol
59, rue Lepic

During the middle of 1899, M. and Mme George Auriol moved to this courtyard building from the nearby rue des Abbesses. They were to stay in this apartment, with a good view of Paris, for four years. Auriol, a talented graphic artist, edited the journal of Le Chat

Noir café, wrote short stories and poems, illustrated and edited books, sketched, painted watercolors, and cut woodblocks. He is perhaps best known today for his Japanese-style woodcuts, his lithographs, and his yearly family Christmas cards.

Filled bookshelves lined the walls of Auriol's large studio room. Publishers in Paris sent him copies of their new books because

> *he was a nice man, sociable, talkative; he talked books, books, books; a small man with a moustache and beard, always a hat on his head; he could be gay and cheerful—he could be mad and furious.*

The stately Mme Auriol was a very traditional French housewife who marketed every morning and kept the household accounts. As the Auriols rarely socialized together, Madame conducted Saturday afternoon tea parties with her women friends, while Auriol met many people during his weekday business activities but remained a loner in social life. A year after his death in 1938, his widow sold the 258 pieces of Auriol's existing art and writings to the Bibliothèque Nationale because she said she needed the money.

20. Residence of Theo and Vincent van Gogh
54, rue Lepic

After a tumultuous eighteen months spent painting, studying and partying with Gaugin, Seurat, and Lautrec, Vincent, battling as always with severe bouts of depression, needed to return to the peaceful peasant fields he loved. The tremendous quantity of brilliantly colored scenes of cornfields, sunflowers, irises, and provençal landscapes resulted from this stay in Aries and St-Remy. A short time after he moved to Auvers, just north of Paris, in 1890, Vincent shot himself in one of his beloved wheat fields. Two months later, Theo suffered a complete mental breakdown and committed suicide in January. The brothers, devoted in life, are buried together in the Auvers cemetery.

Retrace your steps up rue Lepic and turn left on rue Tourlaque.

21. Studio of Renoir
5, rue Tourlaque

The brick building on the corner has what San Franciscans would call a bay window. The top-floor studio was rented by Renoir for space to work on his larger canvasses.

Most of the impressionists were conservative in their political opinions; they were more intent on achieving social and official recognition than in furthering the popular ideas of the avant-garde post-impressionists. When Renoir was invited, in 1882, to participate in a group showing organized by Pissarro (Monet would exhibit only if Renoir did), he wrote:

> *To exhibit with Pissarro, Gauguin and Guillaumin would be as if I were exhibiting with some Socialist group. . . . The public doesn't like anything smelling of politics and I certainly don't want to become a revolutionary. . . . Moreover, these characters know that I took a great step forward in getting accepted by the Salon. . . . Get rid of these people, and give me artists like Monet, Sisley, Morisot, etc., and I am with you. It's not about politics anymore, it's about pure art.*

You are now on the corner of rue Caulaincourt. Turn left for a few buildings.

22. Studio of Henri de Toulouse-Lautrec
27, rue Caulaincourt

When he lived here in 1886, Toulouse-Lautrec filled his dusty studio with oriental objects that reflected the interest of many French artists in Japanese motifs and style. First introduced in 1856 by Félix Bracquemond, Japanese woodcuts were copied and used by ceramicists; later prints by Monet and the portraits of western women in kimonos painted by Whistler, Tissot, and Degas are examples of the influence of oriental art in France. The term japonisme not only describes the art themes, but also the novel oriental tea shops that were opened. Most fashionable Parisian department stores contained Chinese and Japanese specialties.

23. Studios of Toulouse-Lautrec and Steinlen
21, rue Caulaincourt

It was only a short stroll from Toulouse-Lautrec's studio of 1886-97 to the many cafés and cabarets where he found his favorite subjects, the people and the society of the neighborhood. Lautrec met not only his models at the cafés, but also the *femmes de la nuit* whose company he liked. It was in this studio, in 1889, that he painted *La gueule de bois* (*The Chippy*), an oil of his lover of several years, Suzanne Valadon, which depicts her solemnly sitting at Le Rat Mort café, the scene of their initial meeting.

When Steinlen occupied a studio here the structure was especially decrepit, even for le Maquis, and he named it the Cat's Cottage after the large population of cats which not only shared his dwelling but were often the subjects of his drawings. Probably the most famous black cat sketch is on the poster announcing the Tournée du Chat Noir de Rodolphe Salis, the tour throughout France and abroad of the shadow theater of Le Chat Noir. The café was his favorite hangout and he illustrated proprietor Salis's book, *Les comtes du Chat Noir.*

24. Studio of Georges Braque
Rue Caulaincourt, across from Montmartre cemetery

At the time Picasso was painting his monumental modernist painting, *Les demoiselles d'Avignon* (*Women of Avignon*), his friend the poet-critic Guillaume Apollinaire introduced him to Braque, also a painter. The year was 1907 and the revolutionary pre-cubist influence of Picasso can be seen in the work of Braque. It was in his article "Les peintres cubistes," published in 1909, that Apollinaire first named the new movement. During the years 1910 to 1912, the two artists were practically inseparable in their personal and work lives, and this collaboration in analytic cubism makes it impossible to state definitively whether Braque or Picasso first created cubism.

Drafted into the French army in 1914, Braque was so severely injured a year later that he could not work until 1917. He returned here to an old studio and wrote the definitive explanation of cubism, "Thoughts and Reflections on Painting":

> *Limiting the means gives the style, engenders the new form and gives an impulse to creation. . . . It is often limited means that make the charm and the force of primary paintings. Extension, on the contrary, leads the arts to decadence. . . . I love the rule that corrects emotion. . . . I love the emotion that corrects the rule.*

In a passage from *Black Spring* (1936), Henry Miller describes walking along the rue Caulaincourt to Sacré-Coeur. As he rounded a turn in this street, "the sharp swing to the right plunges me into the very bowels of Paris. Through the coiling, sliding intestines of Montmartre the street runs like a jagged knife-wound."

Turn left on rue Joseph-de-Maistre for one block then right on rue Constance.

25. Studio of Fernand Cormon
10, rue Constance

Cormon taught at this beaux-arts studio, one of the original ateliers of the Ecole des beaux arts studio teaching system for French art students that were established in 1863. A celebrated artist directed each studio and by 1883 the system had been modified into commercial teaching studios situated throughout Paris where the professor, who was usually more interested in his own work than in supervising the determined young students, was present about two days a week. The day-to-day teaching was left to a *massier*, a kind of chief student elected by his cohorts.

Toulouse-Lautrec, once the massier in the *atelier libre* (free studio) of Cormon, referred to his *maître*, or teacher, as "the ugliest and thinnest man in Paris." A fine example of Cormon's highly colored mural decorations can be viewed in his ceiling paintings at the Petit Palais. These are very different from the paintings of modern neighborhood life that were executed by his students Toulouse-Lautrec and van Gogh.

Walk left on rue Lepic then right on rue des Abbesses.

26. Studio of Auriol
44, rue des Abbesses

From his fourth-floor studio, Auriol had a view of almost the whole of Paris. A blue Japanese-motif flag hung from the balcony and the large studio room reflected his intense interest in the arts japonais. Stalks of blooming purple irises, the flower of Japan, and lovely rare orchids placed around the room were symbols of Auriol's love of flowers.

In a book written in 1893, Louis Morin described Auriol's work:

He needs a freer field, where his personality can develop itself at ease, with no obligation to obey the requirements of text. This is why he succeeds better than anyone else with the covers of books, magazines, posters, tailpieces, friezes, titles and borderings.

27. Métro Abbesses designed by Hector Guimard
Place des Abbesses

The picturesque art nouveau Métro entrance designed by architect Hector Guimard shelters the 285 steps down to the deepest station in Paris. When the Métro was opened in 1900, the nationalistic Parisians criticized the traditional German olive-green color entrances of glass and wrought-iron arches with amber tulip-shaped lights; they wanted them painted the French tricouleur blue, white, and red. Originally this station stood in front of the city hall (Hôtel de Ville) of Paris but with the remodeling of the place de l'Hôtel de Ville, it was banished to Montmartre. Now it is one of the two station entrances still covered by the original glass roof. The citizens of Paris were not only unhappy about the colors, but many felt the design was too extreme and, consequently, some of the station entrances were replaced by square block structures and the original Guimard designs were sold; one is on display in New York's Museum of Modern Art.

Go north up the hill to the small square.

Hector Guimard's architectural designs for Métro entrances have become part of the romance of Paris. This is Métro Abbesses. (Mary Ellen Jordan Haight.)

28. Formerly Le Bateau-Lavoir
13, rue Ravignan

Art lovers from throughout the world flock to the pleasant tree-shaded place Emile-Goudeau, the former site of an old piano factory thought of by art historians as the Villa Medici of modern art. Because its shape was similar to the laundry boats floating on the River Seine, the dilapidated rabbit warren of studios was fondly referred to as the Bateau-Lavoir (laundry boat). Rebuilt by the city of Paris after a disastrous fire in 1970, the studios are now rented to more prosperous artists.

As seen from the street-level entry, the conception of the size of the building is misleading. The three floors, home to thirty-four various artists in the early years of the twentieth century, descend the steep hill behind. Poets Max Jacob, Pierre Reverdy, and Max Salmon; sculptor Charpentier; artists Modigliani, Juan Gris, Derain, and Fernande Olivier and her lover, Picasso, lived the bohemian life in rooms so flimsily constructed that privacy was unknown; a curtain was all that separated Picasso's studio and Fernande's room. "Love's sighs traveled easily through the partitions," wrote the chronicler of Montmartre, Roland Dorgelès, "and all the more so did the domestic outbursts that could be heard from the hold of the houseboat to the hatchway. Then, Picasso's dogs began to howl . . ." Sharing Picasso's disheveled, dirty studio were a pet mouse living in a drawer and two dogs. Canvasses were strewn everywhere, even on the bed and in the little-used bathtub.

This writer's favorite narrations of bohemian life in the Bateau-Lavoir are contained in the various conflicting versions of the banquet given in honor of the sixty-four-year-old retired *douanier* (customs officer), Henri Rousseau, and his sale of a painting to Picasso. The recollections of the celebration—those by Picasso, Leo and Gertrude Stein, Maurice Raynal, and Fernande Olivier— agree on only *two* facts: the affair *did* happen and it took place in Picasso's studio sometime in the late summer or fall of 1908. Gertrude Stein's account was written twenty-five years post-party and caused such contention that in a 1935 issue of *Transition*, Henri Matisse, Tristan Tzara, Eugène and Marie Jolas, Georges Braque, and André Salmon—the last two having been guests at the affair— produced a "Testimony against Gertrude Stein" in which they complained of her inaccurate memory and falsehoods. You can read the various hilarious accounts of the infamous fête in *Charmed Circle* by James Mellow.

According to Stein, she wore a brown-and-yellow sailor *chapeau*, and Alice B. Toklas had a new hat trimmed with a yellow

Marie Laurencin, Group of Artists, *1908. From left: Picasso, Laurencin, Apollinaire, and Olivier. (The Baltimore Museum of Art, the Cone Collection.)*

feather. The hats were important because, supposedly, a very drunk Salmon ate the yellow feather. By the time the merry guests had climbed the hill, stopping along the way to quench their thirst, they found that Fernande Olivier had neglected to order the banquet food from grocer Félix Potin (The Félix Potin markets can still be seen in Paris) and now the store was closed. Olivier had prepared a large pot of *riz à la valencienne* (Spanish rice), so that became the main course, and she added various dishes from nearby shops.

The guests, besides those already mentioned, included Apollinaire and his mistress, painter Marie Laurencin; Toklas's American roommate from San Francisco, Harriet Weaver; Ramon and Germaine Pichot; Maurice Raynal; and poet Maurice Cremnitz. Picasso and Leo Stein both took credit for organizing the evening and Gertrude later wrote that Apollinaire was responsible for the idea.

As the participants sang and danced for entertainment, Picasso requested that Weaver sing an American song, and when Apollinaire insisted she sing the hymn of the Indian territory, the Californian responded with a well-known cheer of the University of California: "Oski wow!"

According to Laurencin's version, Frédé Gérard, from the nearby Lapin Agile, appeared with his famous donkey, and it is more likely that this animal of odd tastes and voracious appetite devoured the hat trims. Laurencin also wrote that some American tourists visiting the nightlife in Montmartre were attracted by the revelry, whereupon Salmon and Cremnitz "along in the evening" chewed up a bar of soap and began frothing at the mouth in a mad show of delirium tremens. True facts or not, these are the types of tales we relish reading about the wild bohemians of Montmartre.

Continue uphill, turn left at tiny rue de la Mire, and then climb the stairs.

29. Formerly Le Zut
Place Jean-Baptiste-Clément

On the rue Gabrielle side of the place a small gate painted with the word "bière" in black led to this simple café. The floors were dirt and the only furniture consisted of rickety benches.

In the early years, after first arriving in Paris in 1900, a homesick Picasso frequently returned to his native Barcelona. Before he decided to settle in Montmartre, in 1905, his band of fellow Spanish artists created an atmosphere of Spanish life at this ramshackle, squalid, bohemian café. The owner, Frédé (later owner of Le Lapin Agile), wore a béret on his head, sang while playing a guitar, and served beer from the top of a barrel. In an attempt to clean the filthy, cobwebbed walls, the Spaniards white-washed and decorated them with drawings. Picasso's sketch of a hermit surrounded by naked women was named by his Catalan friends "The Temptation of Saint Anthony."

30. Studio of Pablo Picasso and Carlos Casagemas
49, rue Gabrielle

Just short of his nineteenth birthday in 1900, Picasso first arrived in Paris with his friend, painter Casagemas. The two young Catalans from Barcelona were dressed in identical black corduroy suits specially purchased for the trip. After a few days they moved into this studio, then being vacated by the Spanish painter Isidro Nonell. Anywhere but in bohemian Montmartre the short stocky Picasso might have looked strange dressed in a loud checked jacket (replacing the black suit), bright colorful neckties, a cloth cap, and a muffler protecting him against the brisk October weather.

On 25 October the members of the "Spanish ghetto"—that included art critic Miguel Utrillo, Casagemas, sculptor Manolo, and art collector Alexander Riera—celebrated Picasso's birthday. According to Casagemas, they gathered at a café and

we all got drunk. Utrillo wrote nursery rhymes, Picasso made sketches of people, and I wrote verses of 11, 12, 14 and more syllables. There's not a single one who can outdo us in gossiping seriously about people.

31. Residence of Max Jacob
17, rue Gabrielle

After a visit home to Barcelona, Picasso returned to Paris in 1901 for an exhibition in the gallery of Ambroise Vollard. It was a successful showing but, more important, he met Max Jacob. The poet was twenty-five years old and at this time was interested in becoming a painter. "Stick to poetry," Picasso advised, and despite the lack of a common language, the two quickly became close friends.

The short, prematurely balding, intellectual Jacob felt at home with the poets and painters of Montmartre. In one of Picasso's periods of depression, Jacob predicted his future by a palm reading:

All the lines seem to be born from the line of fortune of this hand. Like the first spark in a firework display, this live star-point is only very rarely found, and then only in predestined individuals.

At the end of rue Gabrielle, turn right at the second set of stairs.

32. Place Suzanne-Valadon

Descend the 250 stairs of the rue Foyatier, the most photographed stairway in Paris, to the square that is named for the fine painter Suzanne Valadon. This is a charming place to watch the children on the old merry-go-round in the shadow of Sacré-Coeur or to have a café noir at one of the small cafés across the street.

The Métro Anvers is just two blocks south, by rue Steinkerque, on the busy boulevard Rochechouart.

Stairs descending to place Suzanne-Valadon. (Mary Ellen Jordan Haight.)

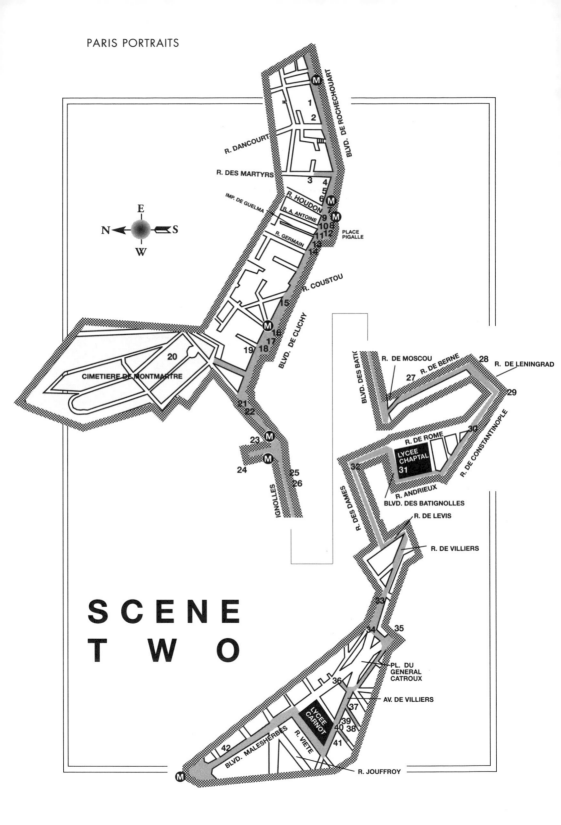

SCENE
TWO

As the night closes in you watch with fascination the gradual streaks of light that crawl out, as avenue after avenue is lighted up, and the whole city is lined out in fire at your feet. . . . The other Montmartre awakens while the quiet inhabitants of the hill go to sleep.

It is a strange grey study in nature, this midnight Montmartre. It is the doing and the done, and the done and the doing. Artists with hope before them, poets with the appreciation of some girl only, and side by side with these the hurried anxious faces of unkempt women and tired-eyed men. . . . It is the aim of Montmartre to stop as long as possible on the térrasse of a café and watch the world go by. To spend an hour in a really typical haunt of the bohemians is a liberal education.
(H. P. Hugh, The Two Montmartres)

In the mid-nineteenth century, the wide new boulevard de Clichy, running from the place de Clichy to the place Pigalle and continuing as the boulevard de Rochechouart, cut through the northern slums of Paris. The slopes of the Montmartre butte were isolated from the flatlands below by the physical boundary, but the large streets also made both areas more accessible. The boulevard de Clichy still retains its sense of a boundary. It is as if all the sleazy bars and questionable forms of entertainment that proliferate here have purposely masked the six- and seven-story buildings of the late 1880s; above and next door to the commercial establishments the aged studios are still visible and still occupied by artists. A walk down the center island among the trees, benches, and old men playing *boules* will enable you to see the buildings on both sides of the busy boulevard.

The original studios consisted of small rooms without running water or gas for lights that were heated, supposedly, by small fireplaces which were often useless since the poor inhabitants lacked money to buy wood or coal. When the evening darkness fell, the isolated individual artist was forced to abandon his work and was happy to escape to the neighboring cafés and cabarets where fellow artists, writers, and poets met and talked. This communication influenced their work.

From 1875, the cafés, cabarets, and bals became central themes in the works of modernists Manet, Degas, van Gogh, Toulouse-Lautrec, and Picasso. They all painted the same subjects—but very differently. These paintings of the avant-garde were rejected by the traditional salons and accepted by only a few galleries, so the cafés became art galleries, where the walls exhibited the latest works of the patrons. The individual theme of each business was carried out in the décor and the illustrated menus. Many of the places published humorous newspapers; today, the pictorial posters by Steinlen and Toulouse-Lautrec are valuable and sought after by museums.

Life, art, and literature before the twentieth century on the Rive Droit can be studied in the history of its studios, cafés, and cabarets. André Warnod wrote in 1923 that "Montmartre is a dead town that lives on memories," but not to imaginative strollers able to eliminate the tackiness and put themselves into the world of a hundred years ago.

Métro Anvers
Buses 30, 54
Walk down the center island that separates the halves of the wide boulevard so you can easily see both sides.

1. Elysée-Montmartre
70–72, boulevard de Rochechouart
Behind the rococo façade existed the prototype of all the great dance halls pictured by the artists in the nineteenth century. Streams of celebrants ventured to the city outskirts to view the new dance, the cancan, in the interior of gilded stucco, velvet hangings, and crimson plush under brilliant chandeliers.

2. Formerly Le Chat Noir and Le Mirliton
84, boulevard de Rochechouart
Rodolphe Salis founded the original "Black Cat" café in 1881 as a place for local poets and musicians to perform in the evenings, creating a light-hearted mood for the customers. For four years, Salis published the weekly newspaper, *Le Chat Noir,* containing poems, stories, tales about café life, write-ups on modern artists, and reviews of exhibitions, all written by the most loyal clientele. Many celebrated artists, such as Steinlen, Rivière, and Willette, drew the humorous caricatures that appeared on the front page.

When Le Chat Noir moved in 1885, it was replaced by Le Mirliton. As Aristide Bruant, the new proprietor, already had a reputation for irritating behavior and vulgar speech, he now saw himself as a rival of the pleasant Salis. No changes were made in the façade and the interior décor. Friday evenings were reserved for the *beau monde* (smart set), as fashionable society found it amusing to hang out with the lower classes and to be insulted by Bruant.

In the move, Salis inadvertently forgot one chair. When he sent for it, Bruant refused to hand it over, and then nailed it to a wall. This fuss became the pretext for a popular ballad:

Oh! Ladies, what a delight it is
to be seated on Louis XIII's chair
It belongs to Rodolphe Salis but to Bruant's you must
go to sit upon it
At the Mirli cabaret
At the Mirli cabaret
At the Mirliton taine tonton
At the Mirliton.

3. Formerly Le Divan Japonais
75, rue des Martyrs

Opened in 1888 with an oriental décor, the café even had Chinese serving ladies. It was here that Yvette Guilbert, the celebrated music hall chanteuse, made her début. In her memoirs, she described the platform on which she performed as being so high at the back of the room that if she raised her arms her hands hit the ceiling. The gas borderlights on the ceiling threw out such heat that the performers' heads were enclosed in a suffocating furnace.

4. Formerly Le Taverne du Bagne
2, boulevard de Clichy

Proprietor Maxine Lisbonne, who had been a prisoner in a Paris jail, decorated the interior with paintings depicting the lives of convicts and soldiers. It was an immediate success, but only for six months of the year 1885–86. People lined up outside to get in, as Lisbonne shouted, "Let another bunch of convicts in!" The waiters, dressed as convicts, must have given slow service as they dragged a ball and chain attached to one leg.

5. Residence of Mary Cassatt
6, boulevard de Clichy

American painter Cassatt settled in Paris in 1874, the same year

Degas saw her work and became her mentor and fast friend. When she exhibited with the male French painters, her impressionist studies of the human figure and of people engaged in simple daily tasks were praised both by fellow artists and critics. From a wealthy Pittsburgh family, it was not unusual for Cassatt to give financial aid to many of the struggling impressionists.

6. Studio of Darius Milhaud
8–10, boulevard de Clichy

Born in Provence, Milhaud became a disciple of Erik Satie and a member of the group of modern composers known as The Six. Satie, impeccably dressed in dark suits and high collars with a monocle in one eye, described his friend Milhaud as slovenly in his dress and his studio as equally disheveled. The prolific Milhaud collaborated with Diaghilev and his Ballets Russes as the arranger of the music for Satie's ballet *Relâche*. To prove his versatility, he once even composed music for the words of a seed catalogue.

Notice the three floors of studios at number 9.

7. Residence of Picasso and studio of Sarah Bernhardt
11, boulevard de Clichy

When Picasso and Fernande Olivier moved from the butte in 1909, his life as an impoverished artist was over because a Russian collector had recently purchased fifty of his works. Although this plush apartment contained both a drawing room and a large studio, Picasso continued to work with his old friends in the decaying old Bateau-Lavoir.

With the change in his economic status, Picasso now purchased a Louis Philippe sofa upholstered in purple velvet, a grand piano, and a large cherry sideboard for the dining room. Age-worn tapestries were hung on the walls. A maid cleaned and cooked the meals, but Picasso was suffering from indigestion—he gave up drinking wine and eating anything other than vegetables, fish, grapes, and rice pudding.

A change in Picasso's painting style absorbed his thoughts, causing him what we would now label stress. During the previous summer in Spain, he saw the Spanish landscape and its villages in the shapes that he later interpreted in paintings defined as classical cubism. Gertrude Stein described this change:

Spaniards know that there is no agreement, neither the land-

Pablo Picasso in his apartment at 11, boulevard de Clichy.

scape with the houses, neither the round with the cube, neither
the great number with the small number, it was natural that a
Spaniard should express this in the painting of the twentieth
century, the century where nothing is in agreement...

She went on to say:

*Cubism is a part of the daily life in Spain, it is in Spanish
architecture. The architecture of other countries always follows the*

31

line of the landscape . . . but Spanish architecture always cuts the lines of the landscape and it is now that is the basis of cubism. . . . Nature and man are opposed in Spain, they agree in France, and this is the difference between French cubism and Spanish cubism and it is a fundamental difference.

Before Picasso moved here, actress Sarah "the divine" Bernhardt, in 1873, occupied a large studio for the sculpting of elaborate pieces. She arrived daily at 10:00 A.M. and, if not required at the theater, she worked until friends arrived for tea. In her piece, *Fantastic Inkwell, Self Portrait as a Sphinx,* she modeled herself as a sphinx crouched behind the inkwell, an ostrich feather plume inserted in her bronze hair. *Art Journal* of 1888 commented that "Madame Bernhardt has been the cause of more art in others than she has produced by her own hand." She was drawn, sculpted, and painted by scores of admirers and worshipped by legions of captivated men. Just before his death in Paris in 1900, Oscar Wilde told a friend that "the three women I have most admired in my life are Sarah Bernhardt, Lily Langtry, and Queen Victoria. I would have married any one of them with pleasure."

8. Formerly La Nouvelle Athènes
Place Pigalle, corner of rue Frochot and rue Pigalle

The interior of the café was described by George Moore, the Irish painter who spent much time here while studying in Paris:

A partition rising a few feet or more over the hats separates the glass front from the main body of the café. The usual marble tables are there. . . . In the morning, eggs frizzling in butter; the pungent cigarette, coffee and bad cognac at five o'clock; the vegetable smell of absinthe after the steaming soup ascends from the kitchen; as the evening advances, the mingled smells of cigarettes, coffee and weak beer.

Around 1890, composers Erik Satie and Maurice Ravel first met at the Athènes. Satie clearly became an important influence on the twenty-year-old Ravel, who later wrote that he considered Satie to be "an awkward and inspired precursor to whom he owed a great deal."

9. Formerly Le Rat Mort
7, place Pigalle

Across the street was the more boisterous "Dead Rat" café. On warm days, customers sat at tables in front of stained glass windows while, inside, the décor was Second Empire. Frequent patrons Degas,

Manet, and Toulouse-Lautrec realistically captured the setting in their paintings, as did the many other artists who portrayed the large mirrors, the shape of the light fixtures, and the decorative drawings that showed the death of the rat.

Opened in 1880, the café closed in 1906 after its clientele changed from artists, writers, and models to the wealthy bon vivants who entertained their female guests in the elegant private dining rooms.

10. Formerly Cirque Médrano
Place Pigalle

According to Gertrude Stein, when Picasso returned to Paris from Spain in 1904, he "commenced to be a little French, that is he was again seduced by France." Instead of only associating with his familiar Catalan cohorts, his companions now included Max Jacob, Guillaume Apollinaire, and André Salmon. The sadness and darkness of his Spanish blue period, depicted in paintings and drawings of dejected beggars and society's suffering, now evolved into circus themes painted in shades of pleasant rose. According to Stein, artists have always liked the circus and its performers; during this time, Picasso and his writer friends met weekly at the nearby circus, on a vacant plot on the place, where they felt flattered that they were accepted by the clowns, acrobats, jugglers, and horse riders. This is now described as his harlequin period. It was at this time that he painted *The Young Girl with a Basket of Flowers,* the initial Picasso purchased by Stein and her brother Leo Stein.

Henri-Patrice Dillon, Reading of the "Sérénade: At the Théâtre Libre, *1889. (Musées de la Ville de Paris by SPADEM 198.)*

11. Théâtre Libre
Rue André-Antoine, off place Pigalle

The small street is named for the founder of the "free theater." Many of the theater programs were drawn by the fine lithographer George Auriol; one, produced in 1889, depicts an image of the Japanese national flower—the chrysanthemum—resting on delicate branches. Yvette Guilbert, one of the principal singers of the Belle Epoque, attended the plays of Ibsen, Tolstoy, and Zola to study the gestures and manners of the finest French actresses.

12. Formerly Abbaye de Thélème
1, place Pigalle

Situated next to Le Rat Mort and La Nouvelle Athènes, this was a literary rather than artistic café like its neighbors. The interior décor of medieval and high gothic was dark, like a small replication of Notre Dame cathedral. Continuing the theme, the waiters were dressed as monks and the waitresses as nuns. The strong odors of cooking wafted through the faux religious setting.

13. Residence of Pierre Puvis de Chavannes
11, place Pigalle

For thirty years, beginning in 1852, this most celebrated Parisian mural painter of the latter half of the nineteenth century conducted a teaching atelier for the study of the live model. Besides the studio, Puvis de Chavannes maintained an apartment consisting of three rooms and a dressing room. The walls were covered with his drawings and paintings, and the furnishings were sparse; a large table, a couch, and a few armchairs.

After 1880, decorative paintings and sculpture on major public buildings played an immense role in the civic pride which is still held by most residents of Paris. The New Sorbonne, the Latin Quarter campus of the University of Paris, was housed in an imposing series of buildings erected in 1885–89. The murals of Puvis de Chavannes dominated the interior decorations; his hemicycle in the main hall covers a huge wall surface and depicts groups of figures, broken at intervals by trees, with the entire mural encompassing scenes of natural landscapes.

The New Sorbonne stood for learning while the nearby Panthéon (formerly a church) represented both religion and the historical heroes of France. It is here that Victor Hugo was buried in 1885. The Puvis de Chavannes murals in the Panthéon were executed in 1888. For his success and recognition in the decorative arts, Puvis de Chavannes was granted the Grand Cross of the Légion d'honneur in 1889, the greatest honor for a living artist.

14. Studio of Henri Rivière
29, boulevard de Clichy

Rivière's excellent woodblocks were inspired by the ancient techniques employed by the Japanese artists. Rivière commissioned his friend Auriol to create for him a personal monogram, or *cachet,* this method of identification having been practiced by the Japanese and Chinese for hundreds of years. The mark could contain the initial letters of a name, an animal, a plant, or a flower. The most famous representation is the three lily petals of the fleur-de-lys used on the possessions of the kings of France. It is usually gold placed on a background of bright blue. At this time in France, marks of identification were used mainly on manufactured products, such as soap, and such marks had identified books since 1462.

Rivière's first edition of woodblock prints were stamped with his Auriol-designed initials "HR."

You can't miss the next location—just look for the red windmill.

15. Le Moulin Rouge
82, boulevard de Clichy

For over a hundred years, the slowly turning sails of a bright red windmill, with stars strung on wires and a partial moon displayed in the sky, have designated the famous Moulin Rouge. The entrepreneurial Zidler brothers and Joseph Oller inaugurated the celebrated music hall on 6 October 1889, the same year Paris hosted the World's Fair. Posters painted by Toulouse-Lautrec, a frequent celebrant, promised "diverse attractions, high-life rendez-vous." The gardens provided open-air entertainment, while inside, the cancan dancers were recklessly enthusiastic.

In the notorious twenties, when Americans flocked to Paris, the Moulin Rouge met their expectations for a loud and naughty atmosphere. Wrote author William Faulkner to his mother in 1915: "Anyone in America will tell you it is the last word in sin and iniquity. It is a music hall, a vaudeville, where ladies come out clothed principally in lipstick."

Henri Toulouse-Lautrec, Quadrille at the Moulin Rouge,
*1892. (National Gallery of Art, Washington, D.C., Chester
Dale Collection.)*

16. Gertrude Stein
Place Blanche

During the winter and spring of 1905–1906, Gertrude Stein
crossed Paris from her Left Bank home to Picasso's Montmartre
studio to pose for her celebrated portrait. She caught the horse-

Pablo Picasso, Gertrude Stein, *1906. (Metropolitan Museum of Art, bequest of Gertrude Stein, 1946.)*

drawn omnibus that took her to the place Blanche since she refused to ride underground on the new Métro system. A climb up the steep hill brought her to the rue Ravignan, and in nice weather she returned on foot to her celebrated atelier at 27, rue de Fleurus, now marked by a plaque installed by the French government.

Picasso posed her sitting in a dilapidated armchair with one of its arms missing, though in the painting, the chair is not seen;

Gertrude's generous figure, dressed in her usual brown corduroy with a loosely draped collar pinned by a coral brooch, completely hid the chair. When friends complained that Gertrude did not resemble the portrait, Picasso shrugged his shoulders and said: "She will." Gertrude loved the picture and later wrote in her book about Picasso: "I was and I still am satisfied with my portrait." The painting was willed by Stein, who died in 1946, to the Metropolitan Museum of Art in New York City.

At number 60 walk through the massive gates of the Villa Plantones for a surprise view of what remains hidden behind the grimy exterior.

17. Studio of Jean-Léon Gérôme
65, boulevard de Clichy

Look up to the top of this four-story building. The large, top-floor, double-height window indicates the studio of the artist Gérôme until his death in 1904. A traditionalist teacher at the Ecole des beaux arts, he was disturbed by the interest in the impressionists. He forbade his students to make quick oil sketches outdoors and considered the impressionists a dishonor to French art.

This was his sculpture studio. A visiting student described being ushered in through a hall and gallery fitted with sculpted groups to the master's large studio filled with great pieces of marble and paintings. Gérôme worked in plaster first, then the pieces were copied by professional marble carvers or cast in bronze.

18. Residence of Anders Zorn
71, boulevard de Clichy

This elegant stone building also has a double-floored atelier at the top. The artist Zorn lived and worked here for eight years until he returned to his native Sweden in 1896. When he moved here, he considered the boulevard a "less noble but more artistic neighborhood." Trained as a sculptor, his paintings, etchings, and prints were executed in an original free-flowing style.

19. Studio of Fernand Cormon
104, boulevard de Clichy

Cormon's private teaching studio-classroom was like many that were run by famous artists for commercial use. A gaunt, thin figure, Cormon gained notoriety for his large and dramatic paintings of prehistoric scenes. His teaching had little influence on the works of the modern students such as van Gogh and Toulouse-Lautrec, who preferred to illustrate realistically the life and residents of the area.

20. Cimetière de Montmartre
Avenue Rachel, off boulevard de Clichy

My favorite walk, especially when it is raining, when it is pouring with rain, is through Montmartre cemetery, which is near where I live. I often go there and I have many friends there. (Hector Berlioz)

Many celebrated artists and writers are buried in this lovely setting: Edgar Degas, Henri Murger, Jacques Offenbach, Hector Berlioz, Alexandre Dumas, Vaslav Nijinsky, and Nadia Boulanger lie in different divisions.

As you enter, first look for Division 4. Impressionist painter Degas evicted a distant cousin from the family tomb to make a place for himself twenty-four years before he would need it. He wanted to make certain there would be room so he could stay in the neighborhood where he was raised. Look for his face on the door of the family crypt where, at the age of eighty-three, in 1917, he was entombed.

In Division 5, a full-size statue of a sad female marks the grave of the writer Henri Murger who died young at thirty-nine. His book *Scènes de la vie de bohème* (1851) describes the intense poverty in which he lived during his short life. Many opera fans have cried over the pathetic suffering of his characters living in cold garrets, and especially the death of Mimi in Puccini's opera *La bohème* (1896).

In 1880, the German composer Jacques Offenbach was buried in Division 9. When just a young boy, his family brought him to Paris in 1833 to study music since he had shown a virtuosity on the cello. Today his satiric and lyrical melodies for the theater still charm music lovers.

A simple black marble monument in Division 20 denotes the grave of composer Hector Berlioz. Preferring to compose for full orchestra, Berlioz's revolutionary, emotional, and colorful compositions express his romantic yearnings. He composed his famous *Symphonie fantastique* (1830) for the Irish actress Harriet Smithson.

In Division 21, Alexandre Dumas, fils, the illegitimate son of the great author of *The Three Musketeers* (1844), was buried in 1895. Dumas, père, tried to discourage his namesake from also writing fiction. The young Alexandre did produce thirteen unsuccessful novels before *La dame aux camélias* (1852) which in 1853 became the basis for Giuseppe Verdi's opera *La traviata*. Elected to the Académie française before his father, the junior Dumas was also awarded the Légion d'honneur.

Along the road in Division 30, look for the Rodin sculpture that is a memorial to the author Stendhal. Supposedly his two lasting regrets were that "he was fat, and that he had been born a commoner and could not console himself for not belonging to the nobility."

A flower-carved tomb in Division 33 belongs to the important musical family of Boulanger. After World War I, many young Americans studied with Nadia Boulanger at the Conservatoire américain in Fontainebleau. Shortly before her death at ninety, her former student Leonard Bernstein inquired about the music she still heard in her mind. Which of her favorite composers did she hear? She replied: "A music that has neither beginning nor end." Also buried here are Boulanger's mother and her sister, Lili, the first woman to win the Prix de Rome for musical composition.

21. Studio of Georges Seurat
128 bis, boulevard de Clichy

From the mid-eighties until his early death in 1891 at the age of thirty-two, Georges Seurat worked from models posing in dim but steady light in this studio. It was in the small, easily portable, meticulously drawn oil studies executed outdoors that he captured direct observations of the neighborhood personalities and their activities. Thus he reconciled the traditional style of his beaux-arts education with the innovations and lessons of impressionism.

22. Studios of Paul Signac and Picasso
130 ter, boulevard de Clichy

Seurat's close friend Signac occupied a studio a few doors away from 1886 to 1888. A founder of the Salon des Indépendants in 1884, Signac was a painter, sailor, political activist, and theorist of neoimpressionism. With Seurat, they transformed impressionism into a systematic and less pragmatic analysis of light by applying thousands of dots of colored paint to form figures and landscapes.

His pointillist painting of the boulevard de Clichy in snow was rendered in 1886.

When Picasso returned to Paris from Barcelona in 1901, he moved into the top-floor flat that had belonged to Carlos Casagemas, who took his own life at L'Hippodrome café next door. The small two-room studio consisted of an entrance hall and bedroom, with the bathroom outside on the sixth-floor landing. Still in great pain over the suicide of his friend and fighting the inner turmoil and demons within himself, Picasso turned to the color blue to express his suffering. His memorial to his dead friend, *The Burial of Casagemas*, the largest canvas of his early years in Paris, was painted here. Surrounded by the sad memory of Casagemas, a depressed Picasso soon longed for Barcelona, and in 1902, at age twenty, he returned there to his parents' home.

23. Café Wepler
Place de Clichy

Henry Miller lived in the suburb of Clichy in the 1930s with fellow writer Alfred Perlès. He often returned to his favorite Montmartre café and the prostitutes he could meet here and on the boulevard.

In *Tropic of Cancer* (1934), he described his life of poverty in his spiritual home—Paris:

> A man does not need to be rich nor even a citizen to feel his way about in Paris. Paris is filled with poor people—the proudest and filthiest lot of beggars that ever walked the earth, it seems to me. And yet they give the illusion of being at home. It is that which distinguished the Parisian from any other metropolitan soul.

24. Formerly Le Guerbois
9, avenue de Clichy

Before 1870, Manet and his friends, including Degas, Renoir, Monet, and Pissarro, gathered at this café on Sunday evenings and on Thursdays around five. The entry room resembled the terrace of any café along the boulevard: all gold and white, full of mirrors and lights. It was the interior room that was unusual—a huge crypt with a low ceiling. Emile Zola, a frequent patron, described the atmosphere in his 1886 work *L'oeuvre*. When the café closed in 1889, it had established its importance in the history of impressionist

41

art because it was here that the first modernist painters formulated the theory of impressionism and planned the 1874 première exhibition of impressionist work.

Return to the bustling place de Clichy and turn right.

25. Residence of Aimé Millet
21, boulevard des Batignolles

The successful sculptor Millet died here in 1891. His major monuments can be seen in the Louvre, the Tuileries, and the Luxembourg Gardens as well as on the façade of the Paris Opéra.

26. Formerly Hôtel Fournet
23, boulevard des Batignolles

Josephine Baker, the celebrated American dancer-singer, and the cast of *La revue nègre,* stayed here in November 1925 while performing at the Théâtre des Champs-Elysées. Baker shared her two-bedroom suite with French poster artist Paul Colin, a parakeet, a parrot, two baby rabbits, a snake, and a baby pig.

Turn left at Métro Rome.

27. Residence of Virgil Thomson
20, rue de Berne

When Thomson first came to Paris as a member of the Harvard Glee Club in June 1921, he fell in love with the city and stayed on to study music with Nadia Boulanger while living here in a fifth-floor apartment. Returning to Harvard in 1922 for three more years, he then came back to Paris and this room.

By 1926, Thomson had become a member of Gertrude Stein's charmed circle, for, as she said, he "was the greatest living master of prosody." While at Harvard, he had experimented with setting parts of her book *Tender Buttons* (1959) to music; and after being introduced to Stein by composer George Antheil, he chose to compose musical settings for her works *Susie Asado* (1922) and *Preciosilla* (1926), thus becoming a close friend.

28. Studio of Edouard Manet
Rue de Léningrad and rue de Berne

In his studio on this corner, the painter Manet, more a traditionalist than an impressionist, made and dwindled away a fortune in his short lifetime of fifty-one years. After his death in 1883, his widow, in financial straits, held a sale at his studio where the 1863 oil *Olympia* did not sell at her price of 10,000 francs ($182). In 1889, Claude Monet organized a subscription to pay 20,000 francs to buy the work for the Louvre. "It is the best homage that we could render to the memory of Manet," he wrote to Zola, "and at the same time it is a discreet means of coming to the aid of his widow." Zola refused to contribute on the grounds that Manet must find his own way to the Louvre. A committee of the national museums agreed to admit the painting to the Luxembourg Museum for public display unless or until the Louvre accepted it. Payment was made to Mme Manet in 1889; and in 1907, twenty-four years after Manet's death, the painting was hung in the Louvre. Today it can be seen in the Musée d'Orsay.

After a right turn on rue de Léningrad, you will see a convergence of busy streets.

29. Place de l'Europe

Gustave Caillebotte's oil on canvas, *The Place de l'Europe, Rainy Day* (1877), details the six arms of the three major thorough-

Gustave Caillebotte, Paris, A Rainy Day, *at place de l'Europe, 1877. (The Art Institute of Chicago, Charles and Mary F. S. Worcester Collection, 1964.)*

fares that cross in this functional square. The figures are shown crossing in a diversity of directions, their umbrellas wet with rain, without apparent communication between the urban dwellers. The cobbled streets and center area are unmarked by any monument. The whole conjunction of streets crosses the tracks of the gare Saint-Lazare by way of an iron bridge.

30. Residence of Guillaume Apollinaire
9, rue de Constantinople

It was Picasso who introduced the "Poet of Paris" to the artist Marie Laurencin with the comment that he had discovered a fiancée for him. Although never formally engaged, the pair was inseparable for the ensuing five years; Laurencin continued to live with her mother and Apollinaire maintained his home here.

When Apollinaire invited Marie to a Gertrude Stein Saturday evening salon Stein found Laurencin to be very young, very chic, and very interesting—an unusual comment for Stein to make about a woman, since at Gertrude's soirées Toklas was assigned to entertain the wives and girlfriends in another part of the room.

In the young Laurencin's 1908 painting, *Laurencin, Apollinaire and His Friends,* she depicts the quintet of Apollinaire and herself, Fernande Olivier, Picasso, and his large white shaggy dog Fricka. Gertrude purchased the simple primitive work, Laurencin's first sale.

Now a right turn.

31. Residence of Charles Angrand
45, boulevard des Batignolles

In 1893, the painter Angrand lived here near his friends and fellow neoimpressionists Seurat and Signac. The term neo-impressionism was coined in 1886 by the critic Félix Fénéon in his account of the eighth impressionist exhibition.

Take a right turn at rue de Rome.

32. Residence of Stéphane Mallarmé
89, rue de Rome

A large plaque marks this as the residence of symbolist Mallarmé from 1875 until his death in 1898. Most of the important French writers, as well as noted Britishers Algernon Swinburne, Oscar Wilde, and George Moore, attended the famous Tuesday parties held in his fourth-floor rooms.

For most of these years, Mallarmé taught English at the Lycée Condorcet, where his students included Marcel Proust and the writer Daniel Halévy, who wrote:

Mallarmé came from his small flat in the rue de Rome . . . and then crossed the place and the pont de l'Europe. Each day, he told George Moore, he was gripped by the temptation to throw himself from the top of the bridge onto the tracks, in order finally to escape the mediocrity in which he was imprisoned.

Turn left on rue des Dames, then right on rue de Lévis and left at rue de la Terrasse.

33. Novel topic of Emile Zola
Avenue de Villiers

In the latter half of the nineteenth century, the ornate brick buildings on the avenue de Villiers contained the deepest concentration of art and wealth in Paris. In his novel *Nana* (1880), Zola describes the typical house of a successful young artist living "in the luxurious quarter":

Built in the Renaissance style by a young painter intoxicated by his first success, who had been forced to sell it as soon as it was ready, it was a palatial building designed on original lines, with modern facilities in a deliberately eccentric setting.

34. Sculptures of Alexandre Dumas, père and fils, and Bernhardt
Avenue de Villiers and boulevard Malesherbes, place du Général-Catroux

This magnificent tree-lined intersection contains a wealth of interesting art. First, next to the Conservatoire municipal Claude Debussy, across Malesherbes, is the reclining figure of the great Sarah Bernhardt with the inscription that it is from "her companions and her admirers." In small parks across from each other are Gustave Doré's monuments to Alexandre Dumas fils and père.

35. Studio of Edouard Detaille
129, boulevard Malesherbes

It was a painting of the studio by Meissonier's seventeen-year-old student Detaille that first attracted the Paris art world to the young artist. Then it was his detailed depictions of Napoléon's military successes in the war against Russia in 1870 that brought him popular acclaim.

36. Residence of Jean-Louis-Ernest Meissonier
131, boulevard Malesherbes

The sale of his extremely expensive battle paintings provided the painter Meissonier with the most elegant and spectacular home-studio in Paris. The large stone building with the air of a cloister proclaimed his wealth and success. According to Albert Wolff:

Rooms, properly speaking, do not exist in this artist's habitation; they are replaced by two studios which connect with each other and occupy the whole width of the first floor; there one of the greatest artists of this century is bent over a labour, which has lasted for fifty years, with the same commitment and passion.

The walls were covered by his sketches, painted studies, and wax models he made in careful preparation for his meticulous and realistic scenes.

Although the most famous artist of his time, Meissonier is practically unknown today. Yet, the *pompier* (conventional) painter was the favorite artist of surrealist Spanish artist Salvador Dali, who was born after Meissonier's death in 1889.

37. Residence of Louis-Ernest Barrias
48, rue Fortuny

The highly successful Spanish sculptor Barrias lived on the street renamed in 1877 for the Spanish painter José María Fortuny, three years after Fortuny's death. Barrias, a teacher at the Ecole des beaux-arts, sculpted pieces that can be seen at the Opéra, the Sorbonne, and the Louvre. In 1902 his bronze *Monument to Victor Hugo* was placed in the place Victor-Hugo at a cost of 250,000 francs.

38. Residence of Bernhardt
35–37, rue Fortuny

Bernhardt's ornate gothic-style house-studio, with large leaded windows and turrets, was constructed in 1877 at a cost of over 500,000 francs. Having become a major actress, her new social and economic standing necessitated moving from Montmartre to the most fashionable area of Paris.

The extensive interior was furnished in exotic pieces, such as a couch covered in small tiger skins. Plants, masks, spears, and a variety of paintings, including life-size portraits of Mme Bernhardt and her son, adorned the walls. The library held extremely rare books, many of them first editions with handmade leather bindings.

It was the menagerie that was Sarah's paramount eccentricity. A friendly lynx held on a leash startled visitors, and a baby tigress was allowed to walk about on the dining table, to the intense discomfort of the dinner guests. Until the odor of the King of Beasts overpowered everybody, a caged lion lived in the corner of her studio.

The great soprano Nellie Melba, after describing the antlers on the walls, the fur rugs, and a stuffed snake under glass, exclaimed:

Side by side with this extraordinary menagerie were busts of Sarah herself, busts of mythological persons, easels, pieces of tapestry, dying plants. . . . I even remember that under one of the tables there was a large bowl of water in which somewhat adipose goldfish swam round and round in their dusty watery world.

Number 37 was demolished in 1960 and number 35 was stripped of its adornments in a public sale in 1970.

39. Musée Jean-Jacques Henner
43, avenue de Villiers

You cannot miss the imposing façade of stone and pink brick with enormous studio windows on the third and fourth floors. Above the entrance is a bronze portrait bust of Henner, whose classical paintings in vogue in the 1880s and 1890s were often based on themes from the writings of Homer, Virgil, Horace, and Ovid. Devoted to study in the Louvre, he was deeply influenced by old masters such as Rembrandt and Titian, yet he admired the work of the young American impressionist Mary Cassatt.

40. Residence of Claude Debussy
58, rue Cardinet

The modern French composer, acclaimed as the father of twentieth-century music, lived here when, in April 1902, his opera *Pelléas et Mélisande* was first performed by the Opéra-Comique.

As a boy of ten, he was admitted to the Paris Conservatoire but rebelled against formal studies and academic rules. Asked what rules he followed, he responded, "My pleasure, my whim." Debussy was influenced early by Wagner and the Russian Moussorgsky, but after meeting Erik Satie he developed a style that was experimental and sensual. Satie claimed that he suggested to Debussy the notion of musical impressionism as a complement to the established art movement and as a movement toward French musical style.

41. Studio of Mihaly Munkacsy
53, avenue de Villiers

The Hungarian painter's studio was *très élégant,* with liveried servants and visits from Parisian high society. He moved to Paris in 1872 and his success attracted a most high-class following. On Fridays, the society artist held open house; it was said that not a Friday passed without at least fifty vehicles of the finest *grand monde* (high society) parked at his door.

42. Residence of Coco Chanel
160, boulevard Malesherbes

"Coco" Chanel was twenty-five when she agreed to live with Etienne Balsan, bon vivant gentleman horse-breeder, who kept bachelor's rooms in this building in addition to a country château near Paris. With hopes that a career in the theater would change the poverty in which she was raised in an orphanage, Chanel left her birthplace, Moulins, in central France, to appear on the stage in Vichy. It was here she met the wealthy Balsan and soon joined his sphere of dilettantes who followed the European racing circuit.

Gowned in a style of her own creation, Chanel stood out in the world of overdressed, bejeweled women; she dressed according to her own taste and comfort in outfits that fluidly skimmed her boyish body instead of covering tight corsets. In 1907, Chanel had cut her thick brown hair in bangs, creating a novel style that would eventually lead to the short bob. On a windy day in 1910, she appeared in a small unadorned boater hat that became the height of fashion and remained so for the next twenty-five years. The influential women around Balsan requested that Chanel design hats for them, and, in her boredom with the life of idleness, she asked to go to Paris to become a *modiste* (milliner). Balsan viewed the idea as a lark, but his best friend, Arthur "Boy" Capel, gave it merit. Instead of providing her with a proper shop, Balsan allowed her the use of his small, ground-floor city apartment. This was a grave error for Balsan, as the encouraging Capel lived nearby and soon replaced him as her lover.

Today the name Chanel is synonymous with good taste and high fashion for, as she said: "Fashion is not simply a matter of clothes; fashion is in the air, borne upon the wind; one intuits it; it is in the sky and on the macadam; it comes from ideas, manners, events."

The Métro Malesherbes is just ahead.

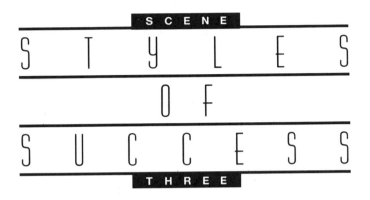

SCENE

STYLES

OF

SUCCESS

THREE

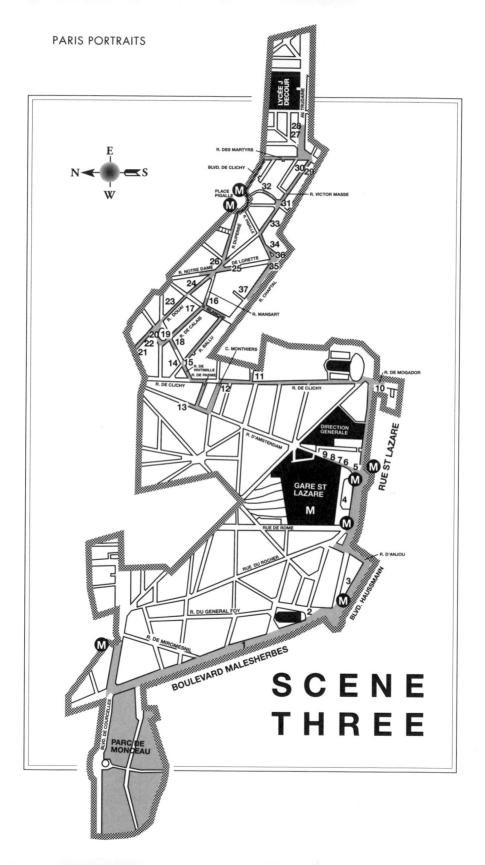

Wealthy and successful artists of the Belle Epoque worked in lavish studios situated north of the Arc de Triomphe and on the elegant tree-shaded streets surrounding the serene park Monceau. Meanwhile, struggling poor urban artists gathered in a disreputable region of bars, brothels, and gloomy hotels south of the boulevard de Clichy. In the labyrinth of narrow streets of lower Montmartre, there were pockets of quiet hamlets on private lanes that were dense with artists' studios. Behind tall metal entrance gates, you can still see the small cul-de-sacs set amidst the lively bustle of crowded streets lined with the cafés where the isolated artists gathered after a day of work.

The third stroll is a journey of contrasts. Whole streets of artists' studios—ranging from the luxurious to the squalor of a single small room without heat, water, or toilet facilities—predominate in certain areas. The densely populated urban setting is portrayed in all its degradation by Degas, Toulouse-Lautrec, and Zola, all of whom lived here.

The *gare* (railroad station) Saint-Lazare served as a vital nerve center of travel and communication. Many of the impressionists either kept studios for working on large projects in the countryside where they lived for a time outside the city or travelled daily by train to the suburbs in order to paint *en plein air*. A study of a timetable listing trains leaving from this station reads like a catalogue of impressionist paintings: Verneuil, Bougival, Rouen, and Le Havre. The railroad was a link to old friends and colleagues and the café life of the boulevards.

Métro Saint-Augustin
Buses 30, 94

From the place Saint-Augustin turn north on boulevard Malesherbes for a couple of blocks.

1. Residence of Isaac Singer
83, boulevard Malesherbes

The name Singer still signifies the sewing machine he first patented in 1851. In order to escape conscription in the army to fight in the Civil War, in 1861 the American Singer moved to France and stayed for the rest of his life. Six years later, with his wife, two-year-old daughter Winnaretta, and year-old son Paris, he moved into a large apartment at this address.

As very wealthy adults, the two children were patrons of the arts. The talented Winnarretta married Prince Edmond de Polignac of an old distinguished French family and hosted a famous musical salon. Paris was a lover of Isadora Duncan and the father of one of her two young children, both of whom drowned in a tragic automobile accident.

Retrace your steps on boulevard Malesherbes.

2. Eglise Saint-Augustin
Place Saint-Augustin

The enormous church, built in 1860–71 by Victor Baltard, has an iron framework that is only visible by stepping inside the stone structure. The metal arches meet to form a great iron dome above the altar. Paintings by Bouguereau decorate the interior, while sculptures by the academician Jouffroy adorn the west façade. In the square in front of the entrance sits Paul Dubois's sculpture of Jeanne d'Arc.

Take boulevard Haussmann to the west.

3. Residence of Marcel Proust
102, boulevard Haussmann

While living here from December 1906 to June 1919, Proust worked on *Remembrances of Things Past* propped in a bed in a room with cork-lined walls. Comtesse Anna de Noailles suggested the padding with cork squares to insure the privacy and quiet he needed to write.

Misia Sert said of the effete snob author (titled society and their mansions obsessed him), who was reputed to speak only to dukes, "The same God who arranged for Molière to draw his last breath on the stage should have allowed Marcel Proust to die at a ball."

The boulevard Haussmann is named for the designer of modern Paris, Baron Georges Eugène Haussmann. During the 1850s, some of the most picturesque portions of old Paris were destroyed in the process of redesigning and widening many of the streets.

Turn left at the next corner and you will see the railroad station ahead.

4. Gare Saint-Lazare

Monet's impressionistic painting of this railroad station led George Moore to write: "When we came to those piercingly

Edouard Manet, Gare Saint-Lazare, *the railroad station, 1873. (National Gallery of Art, Washington, D.C., gift of Horace Havemeyer in memory of his mother, Louisine W. Havemeyer.)*

personal visions of railway stations—those rapid sensations of steel and vapour—our laughter knew no bounds." He was later to admire the painting.

In Ernest Hemingway's short story "My Old Man" (1923), the son and his father moved to suburban Maisons-Lafitte, "the swellest place to live . . . ," and caught the train back home after a day in Paris from this station. Henry Miller, in *Black Spring* (1936), advised the seeker of a prostitute to look in the place in front of the station "if you want to see angels" gathered there.

5. Subject of Camille Pissarro
Place du Havre

From an upper window at the Hôtel Garnier near the place, Pissarro captured on canvas the fleeting figures and bustling carriages on the busy street below in front of the station.

Walk just north around the corner of rue d'Amsterdam to the first café across from the station.

Camille Pissarro, Boulevard des Italiens, Morning, Sunlight. *(National Gallery of Art, Washington, D.C., Chester Dale Collection.)*

6. Formerly Café Criterion
Rue d'Amsterdam

In the winter of 1903–1904, the café was the setting of the momentous meeting of twenty-three-year-old Picasso and Guillaume Apollinaire, "the Poet of Paris." A fast friendship developed quickly; their next meeting was vividly reported by Picasso's friend, poet Max Jacob.

> *He [Apollinaire] was an imposing young man with a deep chest and heavy limbs. . . . He changed in an instant from childlike laughter to pale gravity. The three of us left together and Guillaume carried us off for a stroll which never came to an end. . . . Here began the best days of my life.*

7. Residence of Jules Romains
Rue d'Amsterdam

Romains lived in an apartment near the café Criterion when he met some of his friends (named *copains,* meaning pals, after a book of his by that title) at a bistro in a rough neighborhood near the Père-Lachaise cemetery where he was to be buried in 1972. Always a practical joker, the handsome French novelist pulled a hat low over one eye and was the last of the group to be recognized. The character of this group of friends, which included bookstore proprietors American Sylvia Beach and French Adrienne Monnier, demonstrated Romains's doctrine of *unanimisme,* in which the spirit of the individual becomes a part of the spirit of the group or the country. To demonstrate his doctrine, in his grand novel *Mort de quelqu'un* (*Death of a Nobody*), published in 1911, as the protagonist's funeral procession winds through the streets of Paris, his spirit becomes a part of the lives of his neighbors and thus an eternal element of the city.

8. Residence of Charles Baudelaire
22, rue d'Amsterdam

In 1860, a depressed Baudelaire lived in this third-floor apartment as he struggled with his translation of the tales of Edgar Allan Poe. The perfectionist poet had a neurotic and eccentric personality, having spent years writing one book of verses. His influence on future poets was enormous.

The bedroom of Marcel Proust. (Musées de la Ville de Paris by SPADEM 198.)

9. Residence of Alphonse Daudet and Marie Rieu
24, rue d'Amsterdam

The building appears much as it did in 1857 when the teenage writer Daudet and the almost-twice-his-age Rieu moved in. Daudet described their relationship in his thinly disguised autobiography *Sapho* (1884), subtitled *Parisian Manners*. In the book, Marie sees the building first: "Three rooms and a big balcony. . . . It's a tall building, five floors" (a sixth has since been added). The kitchen and the sitting room opened onto a back courtyard, permeated with the smells of the tavern. The bedroom faced on the noisy street with the jolting of wagons, cabs, and buses shaking it day and night. The comings and goings of the gare across the street added to the din.

10. Théâtre Mogador
25, rue de Mogador

When the renowned dancer Isadora Duncan presented her final stage performance here in 1917, her body was overweight and abused by alcohol, but to the many friends and admirers filling the hall she was still a dynamic presence as she stood on the stage "dancing" with her arms. Duncan's death that year in Nice was as melodramatic as her life. Exclaiming, "Good-bye, my friends. I am going to glory!" she dramatically drove off with a young Frenchman in a dazzling Bugatti sports car. Immediately, the long, flowing, red silk scarf thrown around her neck became entwined in a wire-spoked wheel and fatally broke her neck.

The Gershwin brothers, George and Ira, arrived in Paris on 28 March 1928 to hear George's composition *Rhapsody in Blue* performed here by the Pasdeloup Orchestra, conducted by Rhené-Baton. The Parisian audience went wild, but the composer, fearing the worst, had fled to the bar before the cheering began; however, he returned quickly to respond with a bow from the stage.

From the square de la Trinité proceed north on the rue de Clichy and notice number 28 where the writer, musician, and illustrator Georges Enesco lived from 1908 until his death here in 1955.

Turn right on rue Moncey.

11. Studio of Claude Monet
17, rue Moncey

When Monet painted in a studio here in 1878, his style of impressionism was descended from the naturalists and japonisme, combined with techniques he learned from Manet, Corot, and Courbet. His portrait of Mme Monet is startling: not only does it show the influence of strong Japanese color, but she is dressed in a rich Japanese robe. The life-size work projects a feeling of movement of the large fan she holds in her hand with many open

Claude Monet, La Japonaise, Camille Monet in Japanese Costume. *(Museum of Fine Arts, Boston, 1951 Purchase Fund.)*

fans surrounding in the background. This painting was a strong departure from Monet's delicate realistic landscapes of the French countryside and gardens.

Go back to rue de Clichy, turn right, then go left through the short, picturesque cobblestone street of the *cité* (literally, a housing estate).

12. Théâtre de l'Oeuvre
55, rue de Clichy, Cité Monthiers

Many artists earned money by associating with the theater, in particular the Nabis group of St. Denis, Bonnard, and Vuillard, who designed sets, costumes, and programs for Lugne-Poe's tiny theater. Their work combined decorations and paintings for the public theater, but their interests did not extend to producing works for civic buildings, parks, and monuments.

One of the most sensational productions in this theater was the April 1896 début presentation of Oscar Wilde's *Salomé*. Six years later, the Richard Strauss opera of the play opened in London.

Continue along the short street to the end, exit through the wood door, and turn right to the next corner.

13. Studio residence of Edouard Manet
(77), rue d'Amsterdam

For four years, until his death in 1883, Manet lived in the conventional studio that formerly stood here. The conservative environment did not reflect the scandal his pre-impressionistic works caused among art critics. While busy painting one day, he was visited by an English art critic. Stopping in front of the painting *The Skaters,* he asked of Manet: "That's very fine, but don't you think, Monsieur Manet, that the figures look as though they were dancing, and that the contours aren't sufficiently well-defined?"

"They're not dancing, they're skating," responded Manet, "but you're quite right, they are moving, and when people are moving I can't paint them as though they were standing still."

14. Nadia and Lili Boulanger
36, rue Ballu, place Lili Boulanger

After ninety-two-year-old Nadia Boulanger's death, newspaperman Ned Rorem described her as the most influential teacher since Socrates. Rorem wrote: "Myth credits every American town with two things, a ten-cent store and a Boulanger student." For nearly sixty years, young American musicians flocked to Paris and to Nadia's summer program in Fontainebleau. Nadia said of herself:

> *There were three kinds of music students, the kind who had money and no talent, and those she took; the kind who had talent and no money, and those she took; and the kind who had money and talent, and those she never got.*

American composers Aaron Copland, Virgil Thomson, and Roy Harris were among her students, as well as performers Yehudi Menuhin, Maurice Gendron, and Noel Lee. Supposedly, she spoke to Leonard Bernstein, one of the last of her students, a few days before her death. She believed that American students in the twenties were like Russians in the 1840s: poorly trained but exploding with enthusiasm. Her goal was to correct the former deficit.

Nadia and her younger sister, Lili, lived here from 1904 until their deaths. After Lili died quite young in 1918, Nadia ceased composing to devote herself to teaching and giving a few performances as organist or orchestra conductor.

15. Residence of Emile Zola
23, rue Ballu

At the housewarming for Zola here on Wednesday, 3 April 1878, his friends, including authors Alphonse Daudet and Gustave Flaubert, were served a gourmet grouse dinner. Edmond de Goncourt described the new apartment: "a bedroom with a carved four-poster bed and twelfth-century stained-glass walls and ceilings, altar frontals over the doors, a whole houseful of ecclesiastical bric-a-brac." In this eccentric milieu Zola perched on a Portuguese throne of Brazilian rosewood while writing such novels as *L'assommoir* (1877).

16. Residence of May Alcott
11, rue Mansart

The sister of American novelist Louisa May Alcott lived here during the year 1877. The two sisters had visited Paris together several years before and now Louisa May was supporting her sister May's quest for a career in art.

17. Residences of Hector Berlioz and Arnold Bennett
4, rue de Calais

Berlioz died on 28 March 1869 in this building where Bennett lived from 1903 to 1906 while working on *The Old Wives' Tale* (1908). After Somerset Maugham came to tea in March 1905, Bennett wrote in his journal that Maugham drank two cups of tea, ate biscuits quickly, almost greedily, and smoked two cigarettes furiously. When he asked Maugham if he liked living in the Montparnasse quarter, he replied, "Yes, the atmosphere of it is rather like Oxford."

18. Studio of Monet
20, rue de Vintimille

In 1879, Monet moved his studio here. He also had a home in the suburb of Argenteuil on the River Seine where others of the impressionist group regularly visited him. Monet was concentrating on painting sky and water, along with the subtle effects of light. His subject matter during this period was principally the river and he usually worked from a boat acting as a floating studio.

19. Place Adolphe-Max, square Hector-Berlioz

The picturesque square always has pigeons perching on Berlioz's figure. Here is a good place to sit and watch Parisian mothers with children and the people on their way to the morning market. Even with refrigeration and freezers most French buy fresh food daily.

20. Residence of Eugène Boudin
11, place Adolphe-Max

Boudin was a great influence on Monet in his early years. The son of a sailor, Boudin excelled in views of Normandy beaches and plein-air paintings of light, water, and groups of people. The year following his death in 1898, a retrospective held at the Ecole des Beaux-Arts comprised 304 paintings, 73 pastels, and 20 watercolors.

21. Studio of Tony Robert-Fleury
69, rue de Douai

The celebrated Salon painter taught at the Académie Julian and worked in his private studio here. The painter Marie Bashkirtseff, a student at the academy, recalled: "It is on Saturdays that M. Tony Robert-Fleury comes to the studio, the painter whose *Last Day of Corinth* was purchased by the state and placed in the Luxembourg Museum." He became more than her tutor, as he was involved in her personal development and worldly progress.

22. Residence of Pierre Bonnard
65, rue de Douai

Bonnard's lovely paintings capture the light and excitement of the ordinary life of Paris. When living here in 1905, he painted his optimistic view of the city in a style derived equally from impressionism, Japanese prints, Gauguin, and his lessons at the Académie Julian. The striped wallpaper of his studio was covered with paintings, and more were stacked against the walls. For his paintings, posters, theater designs, and book illustrations, he first recorded his impressions of the city's streets, gardens, and inhabitants in a loose drawing style and then he completed the brightly colored, light-filled works inside his atelier.

Pierre Bonnard in his studio at 60, rue de Douai between 1905 and 1910. (Musée d'Orsay.)

23. Residences of Pauline Viardot and Ivan Turgenev
50, rue de Douai

When the French novelist George Sand visited the opera singer Pauline Viardot at her home here, Charles Dickens, after a greatly anticipated meeting arranged by Viardot, noted his pronounced disappointment with Sand:

> I suppose it to be impossible to imagine anybody more unlike my preconceptions than the illustrious Sand. . . . Chubby, matronly, swarthy, black-eyed. . . . A singularly ordinary woman in appearance and manner.

For thirty years, beginning in 1847, the Russian writer Ivan Turgenev occupied a third-floor apartment, with walls upholstered in fabric and crowded with varying objects. According to Alphonse Daudet, "Turgenev had borrowed the artistic tastes of his friends: music from the wife, painting from the husband" (the Viardots). What is perhaps his most illustrious novel, *Fathers and Sons* (1862), was written here.

24. Residence of André Breton
42, rue Fontaine

The high priest of surrealism lived here for a few years before he moved to the Left Bank. First intending to become a doctor, Breton served as an "auxiliary doctor" in World War I, but upon returning from the conflict, devoted himself to literature. He did not lose his interest in psychiatry, especially not Sigmund Freud, whose theories greatly influenced him when he defined surrealism in the *Manifeste du surréalisme* (1924).

With Louis Aragon and the poet and novelist Philippe Soupalt, Breton founded the review magazine *Littérature* in March 1919. Adrienne Monnier, the proprietor of an important French Left Bank bookshop situated on the rue de l'Odéon, said of the magazine:

> Never, truly, has one seen a table of contents as sensational as that of the first number: André Gide, Paul Valéry, Léon-Paul Fargue, almost all the great loves of the Rue de l'Odéon. And also, Max Jacob, Pierre Reverdy, Blaise Cendrars—the dear fauves [French artists, including Cézanne, pre-cubists].

In 1920, *Littérature* became the organ of the dada movement and in its second issue the first contribution of dadaist writer Tristan Tzara, a Rumanian by birth, was a poem. The May issue contained "Twenty-three Manifestos of Dada."

25. Residences of Edgar Degas and Henri de Toulouse-Lautrec
19 and 19 bis, rue Fontaine

Number 19 bis was described by Degas in an undated letter to Alexis Rouart as "the most beautiful apartment on the third floor to be found in the whole *quartier*." When Degas lived here between 1879 and 1886, the neighborhood was a vital source of subjects for his paintings. With expert academic techniques, in a blend of the opposing forces of tradition and modernity, he sketched outdoors, then completed the work in his studio.

Referring to his painstaking method of working, Degas wrote to Rouart in 1873: "I have never done with finishing off my pictures and pastels." Owners of his paintings were often reluctant to lend them back to the artist for fear that he might continue to perfect his work.

A year after Degas moved out, Toulouse-Lautrec lived next door at number 19, in the home of Dr. Henri Bourges, and, appropriately, painted in the studio vacated by Degas, a great admirer of his work.

26. Residence of Georges Bizet
22, rue de Douai

Not only artists of the late nineteenth century, but composers such as Bizet, who lived here, were influenced by japonisme. Although Bizet never visited the Far East, he had a natural instinct for its rhythms. His love of the East moved him to write *Carmen* (1874) for, as Victor Hugo stated, "Spain is still the Orient!"

27. Formerly L'Auberge du Clou
30, avenue Trudaine

The country-Swiss interior of the Auberge was where Erik Satie first met Debussy. Commented Satie about that fateful union: "The moment I saw him I felt drawn to him and wished I might live at his side forever. And for thirty years I was fortunate enough to see my wish fulfilled."

The best friends exchanged ideas, helped each other ascertain a point of view, and began composing operas based on plays of Maeterlinck. Debussy, four years older than Satie, with many friends among writers and painters, was already familiar with impressionism. When he was awarded the prestigious Prix de Rome in 1885, the tribunal wrote of his piece *Printemps* that it showed "forgetfulness of the importance of preciseness in line and form" and a "vague impressionism" which endangered the "truthfulness" of a work of art.

28. Formerly La Grande Pinte
28, avenue Trudaine

When the "Large Pint" (presumably of beer) opened to the public in 1878, it was the first artistic café in Montmartre. The proprietor, Laplace, a dealer both of art and secondhand goods, covered the walls with paintings, drawings, and his collection of artists' palettes. In 1878 Pissarro added his palette depicting a peasant couple loading a sack of potatoes onto a cart. During the years 1878 through 1880 Manet met here with friends and painted a palette, *Le bock sur une palette* (*The Glass of Beer on a Palette*).

29. Residence of Paul Eudel
9, rue Victor-Massé

The historian Eudel lived here from 1885 until 1895. His best-known work is the history of the Hôtel Drouot, the Paris mansion that is now the famous auction house.

30. Formerly Le Chat Noir
12, rue Victor-Massé

Rodolphe Salis moved his cabaret to this private home in June 1885. Each of the rooms on the three floors was given a pretentious name, such as the room of state or the room of celebrations. The walls were decorated with works drawn by the patrons, and he catalogued his fine collection in a guide to the Chat Noir. Upon Salis's death in 1897, the collection was auctioned off.

The room of celebrations contained depictions of the performances of the shadow theater initiated by Salis and managed by his friend Rivière. Forty-three plays, written by nineteen artists, were performed from 1887 to 1896. When Salis retired in 1892, the shadow theater continued to perform in France and abroad.

31. Bertha Weil gallery
25, rue Victor-Massé

When the twenty-one-year-old Picasso returned to Paris from Barcelona in 1902, he briefly shared a small room with the Spanish painter Joseph Rocarol. When their money was all spent, Picasso sold a painting of Rocarol's to the art dealer Weil for twenty-five francs, enough to pay for their room and food for a few more days, then they went their separate ways.

A new show at the Weil gallery exhibited a few of the paintings Picasso hoped would provide new financial support. Although none of the works were sold, the preface to the catalogue praised Picasso's "indefatigable ardor to see and show everything" and the "wild light" that permeated his work.

32. Residence of Toulouse-Lautrec
5, avenue Frochot

Still in his beloved neighborhood just a short distance from the Moulin Rouge, in 1897 Toulouse-Lautrec continued to portray the bustling area and its unusual residents. Throughout his working life, he produced over 1,000 paintings, 5,000 drawings, and more than 300 prints and posters, most of them depicting the nightlife of Montmartre.

33. Studios of Degas and Auguste Toulmouche
37, rue Victor-Massé

This part of the street overlooks avenue Frochot and a complex

Edgar Degas on the boulevard de Clichy about 1910. (Bibliothèque Nationale.)

of studios in gardens behind private gates. The fashionable painter Toulmouche moved from here to the Left Bank area of Montparnasse around the turn of the century and established a hamlet of artists' studios in a similar sylvan setting.

When art enthusiasts remember Degas, it is generally his paintings, drawings, and delicate sculptures of ballerinas they acknowledge. The son of a banker, Degas lived and worked in the Montmartre area for twenty years. From 1862, when he met Manet, until he died nearly blind in 1917, his work depicted modern urban life in Paris. As closely involved as he was with the impressionists, his work lacked their spontaneity; everything was carefully planned in his intricate drawings of the human figure. In his masterful technical oils, pencil and charcoal drawings, and pastel watercolors, he combined the opposing forces of traditional and modern art.

The sharp-tongued Degas lived a solitary life after he moved here in 1886. As an example of his harshness, artist Berthe Morisot wrote: "Everyone is sufficiently kind enough not to make me feel any regrets, except of course Degas, who has a supreme contempt for anything I do."

34. Residence of Auguste Renoir
64, rue de la Rochefoucauld

At the time of Renoir's residency in 1897, this was described as a street of "gaunt, shuttered, pale-yellow" buildings. His son Jean Renoir quotes his father's instructions to young artists:

Go and look at what others have produced, but copy only nature itself. If you copy, you are assuming a creative personality which is not your own. Nothing that you did would ever be your own. . . . To be an artist you must learn to know the laws of nature.

35. Formerly Le Grand Duc
52, rue Pigalle

Langston Hughes, the American poet, first worked here in 1924 as a dishwasher and then as a waiter. Performing at the cabaret at that time were important blues musicians Cricket Smith and Buddy Gilmoure.

After American jazz was introduced to Parisians and Josephine Baker first danced the Charleston in 1925 in *La revue nègre,* the French were fascinated by the American black culture. French intellectuals and sophisticates danced wildly to the savage rhythms; blacks and whites mixed casually. English heiress Nancy Cunard and American jazz pianist Henry Crowther lived together, and Cole Porter accompanied red-haired black nightclub owner Bricktop to the exclusive Paris Opéra Ball, where she appeared wearing the same Molyneux creation as Princess Marina of Greece.

Cross the intersection to the southern corner.

36. Formerly La Rochefoucauld
On the corner of rue de la Rochefoucauld and rue Notre-Dame-de-Lorette

One of the oldest in Montmartre, the Rochefoucauld café was frequented by both artists and critics. The square main room, furnished with green moleskin wall-sofas and about fifteen marble tables, seated sixty patrons. A spiral staircase led to the rarely used billiards room; dominos was the favorite game of the artists. After working in the morning, Degas took lunch here every day.

Turn around and take the first street west.

37. Musée Renan-Scheffer
16, rue Chaptal

The charming house in the rear of a courtyard and garden is reached through a passage of ivy-covered walls. It is a surprise to discover this quiet idyllic setting in the midst of noisy, teeming lower Montmartre.

Now the museum of literature and artists of the nineteenth century, this was formerly the home of the artist Ary Scheffer. It was constructed in 1820, and ten years later Scheffer began his thirty-year residency. On Friday evenings some of the greatest figures in the arts and letters—Delacroix, Liszt, Chopin, and his lover George Sand—gathered with their friend. In 1856, Ernest Renan married Scheffer's niece. Their daughter and her husband donated the building to the French state in 1956 and since 1962 the lovely Italianate house has been preserved as a museum.

George Sand lived nearby and, in 1923, her daughter contributed a Sand collection consisting of 170 paintings, furniture, jewels, and souvenirs. You can visit every day, except Monday, from 10 A.M. to 5:30 P.M. Definitely worth seeing.

At the end of the street, turn right on rue Blanche to the place Blanche and the Métro.

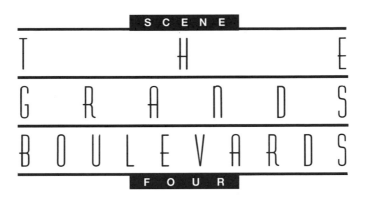

SCENE

THE
GRANDS
BOULEVARDS

FOUR

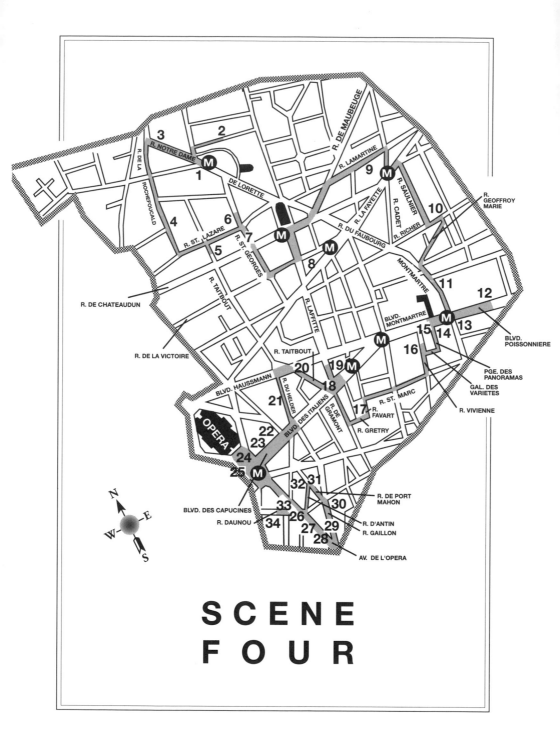

SCENE FOUR

The Grands Boulevards, or great avenues, were created by Baron Georges Haussmann in his dramatic remodeling of Paris in the 1850s, when many of the meandering, medieval cobblestone streets were replaced by exceedingly wide straight avenues. Also radically altered were the famous views of Paris. Previously the busy courtyards of buildings were the focal points of domestic activity, presenting a closed-in appearance of intimacy; now the views from high balconies on fifth and sixth floors provided the observer with vistas of mass activity. The previous close detail of the courtyard gave way to a generalization, contrasting the individual viewpoint and space with a dynamic sweeping panorama of thousands of dwellings, actions, and beings in a single sweep of the eye.

Impressionist technique with its plethora of rhythmic brushmarks was not particularly suited to capture individual detail, but it was a brilliant method for displaying the general activity on the boulevards in which the figures, trees, and buildings almost lose their form completely. For the individual artist the viewpoint and format of the buildings remained constant, but the city changed with the light and with the activities of the inhabitants.

> *Once he sets foot there, the man of active mind might as well write off his whole day. It is a dream of gold, a distraction which you cannot hope to resist. You are in a crowd, yet all alone. (Balzac)*

Métro Saint-Georges
Buses 74, 67

Exit place Saint-Georges, turn left on rue Notre-Dame-de-Lorette. In the center island is a bust of Covar placed by the Société des Peintures-Lithographes.

1. Residences of Lucien Lévy-Dhurmer and "Musette"
3 bis, rue La Bruyère

Algerian native Lévy-Dhurmer, a symbolist painter of innovative and accomplished skill, was described in 1897 as being small in size

> *with close-cropped hair and fair, curly beard, a keen and piercing glance, and the simplest and most unostentatious manners, quick and witty in conversation, evidently by nature meditative and strong-willed. (Milner,* The Studios of Paris*)*

In Henri Murger's romantic novel, *Scènes de la vie de bohème* (1851), the character Musette entertained once a week with receptions held here in her lovely drawing room.

These receptions were like most Parisian receptions with the difference that here everyone enjoyed himself; when there was no place left to sit down, they sat on each other, and it was often necessary for two people to use the same glass.

2. Shop of Julian-Français (Père) Tanguy
14, rue Clauzel

When the first impressionists were either ignored or reviled, Tanguy admired and championed their work. Many of the neighborhood painters purchased supplies here in Tanguy's shop, where he tried to act as an art dealer for the later post-impressionists whom no established dealer would represent. He was the exclusive agent for Cézanne and, when van Gogh lived nearby in 1886, Tanguy spent many hours with the troubled Dutchman.

In 1887, van Gogh painted the famous portrait of his friend Tanguy that now hangs in the Musée d'Orsay. In it Tanguy is seated, hands joined in his lap, wearing a large wide-brimmed hat, directly facing the viewer. After Tanguy's death, this painting was sold by his daughter to sculptor Auguste Rodin.

3. Studio of Eugène Delacroix
54, rue Notre-Dame-de-Lorette

Delacroix's studio inside this beautiful building was pictured in 1852 in an illustration by E. Renard as an immense cluttered room lighted by a large north-light window covering a wall and part of the ceiling. A small stove—an essential in the studios because of the high heat loss through the great expanse of glass—stands in front of the window. In the clutter of paint boxes, palettes, and easels there is only one comfortable chair and sofa, and paintings fill one wall and five easels. Jules Breton, a fellow painter, described Delacroix as having a head "like a sick lion's" and as "a genius who must always remain alone."

Turn right onto rue de la Bruyère, then left at the first street.

4. Musée Gustave-Moreau
14, rue de la Rochefoucauld

Formerly the home and studio of symbolist artist Moreau, the quietly elegant building houses oil paintings, watercolors, draw-ings, and sketches. Check around the side of the building where you can barely see, on the two top floors, the north-light studios with windows overlooking the garden of the adjacent building. Inside, the studios are connected by a simple spiral staircase of rococo charm.

The building presents a model for a wealthy painter's studio, but Moreau, in the 1880s and 1890s, exhibited and sold few works.

The interior staircase of the Musée Gustave Moreau, previ-ously Moreau's home. (La Réunion des Muées Nationaux.)

A great proportion of his output remains on exhibit and is stored here. The top studios house the large canvasses and the small rooms below have wood-panelled walls behind which are whole walls of hidden cabinets that Moreau designed for storage of his smaller works.

As you will observe, Moreau was not interested in depicting the life around him, like his friend Degas, for his works represent subjects from the scholarly study of classical literature and religion. As are most Paris museums, this one is closed on Tuesday, but every other day the hours are 10–12 A.M. and 2–5:15 P.M.

5. Residence of William Saroyan
74, rue Taitbout

From November 1960 to summer 1961, Saroyan lived on the fifth floor of this building back of the Opéra. In his autobiography, *Here Comes, There Goes, You Know Who* (1962), he describes his rooms:

> *This is an ice-cold flat, and while there is a butane heater on rollers to light and to move around in here from place to place, and a small electric heater to plug in I prefer the cold, but such matters are really none of my business at this time.*

6. Studio of Auguste Renoir
35, rue Saint-Georges

In a remark to Henri Matisse, Renoir said: "When I have arranged a bouquet for the purpose of painting it, I always turn to the side I did not plan." The large glass walls of this studio allowed the rectangular room to be flooded with light, which meant that his models—human or plant—could be painted indoors in direct sunlight. Against the light grey walls were stacks of canvasses. The only furnishings were two easels, a couple of cane chairs, two decrepit armchairs covered in a faded flowered fabric, a sad old couch upholstered with material so worn that the original color could not be ascertained, and a white wooden table holding tubes of colors, brushes, bottles of oil or turpentine, and spattered paint rags.

Renoir regularly started work at 8 A.M., pausing occasionally for a cigarette while the model rested. At noon he lunched in a small *crémerie* (dairy) across the street, then returned to work until 5 P.M., when his friends, such as the poet Stéphane Mallarmé, visited.

7. Studio of Sarah Bernhardt
Rue Saint-Georges

Around 1873, while her new studio on the boulevard de Clichy was being prepared, the great tragédienne cum sculptor kept an atelier somewhere on this street. The multimillionaire Baron Adolphe de Rothschild commissioned Bernhardt to sculpt his head, promising to pay a fat fee. After a few sittings, she showed him the clay model before it was to be cast in bronze. With check in hand, Rothschild critically examined the head and yelled, "Is that supposed to be me?" Bernhardt, screaming in rage, grabbed the check, tore it up, then, seizing her work, threw the bust to the floor, where it smashed into pieces.

8. Couture house of Jacques Heim
48, rue Laffitte

The house of Heim is the oldest Paris fashion house still managed by family members in direct descendency. The business was first begun in 1898 by Isidore and Jeanne Heim as a fur venture, but under the direction of their son Jacques, who joined the business in 1925, a design department for suits, coats, and evening dresses was opened. Cubist art was the inspiration for young Jacques's première couture collection. When Heim introduced the first cotton sarong-style bathing suit, inspired by the Tahitian exhibits in the Paris Colonial Exhibition of 1931, he created what *Harper's Bazaar* called "an international style furor." By 1934, the fashion house was so successful it was moved to larger quarters on the avenue des Champs-Elysées.

9. Formerly Paris *Tribune*
5, rue Lamartine

The first edition of the *Chicago Tribune,* European Edition, appeared in January 1919. It particularly reflected the ideas and way of life of the American expatriates drawn to the Left Bank society of Montparnasse. Many of the top names in American newspaperdom served their apprenticeship on the Paris paper. According to Waverly Root, a *Tribune* staffer for thirteen years,

> *the kinds of young men who were drawn to Paris when it was the center of a lively cultural life were also the kinds of young men who were likely to achieve a certain eminence anyway, whether they had passed through the mill of the Tribune or not.*

The notorious Henry Miller worked in the proofroom without writing a line for the paper. His good friend Alfred Perlès, the prototype for Carl in *Tropic of Cancer* (1934), recommended him for a job when they shared a small hotel room on the Left Bank. Miller did not last long, and Perlès must have been speaking only for himself when he wrote in *My Friend Henry Miller* (1956) that their proofreading period was the "most highly fertile of our life in Paris."

After two years as the editor of his college newspaper, William Shirer, in 1925, talked his way into a job with the *Tribune* as a beginning copywriter, for which he was paid $60 a month. Two years later he was promoted to foreign correspondent and moved to London.

When James Thurber was a staff member, he wrote: "The Paris edition of the *Chicago Tribune* was a country newspaper published in a great city." Thurber, who later wrote for *The New Yorker,* was described as "a lonely owl-eyed man with thick glasses."

In 1934 the paper folded and was absorbed by the rival Paris *Herald* (European edition of the New York *Herald Tribune*), creating the New York *Herald Tribune,* European Edition. Now it is the *International Herald Tribune.*

10. Théâtre des Folies-Bergères
32, rue Richer

Two young midwestern American women became the toast of Paris after débuting at the Folies. In 1892, Loïe Fuller, "la belle américaine" from Chicago, wearing unusually filmy costumes of yards of loose flowing silk, performed four dances with colored lights spotlighting her lithe figure. The novel lighting effects revolutionized stage illumination, and the applause and curtain calls lasted for about a half hour, after which Fuller collapsed from exhaustion. Critics declared her "a wizard of light, color, motion, and impressionism." Along with another American, Isadora Duncan, Fuller is considered to be one of the mothers of modern dance.

Very shortly after Fuller died in 1928, Josephine Baker arrived from St. Louis and took Paris by storm when she danced to American jazz while clad in scanty, sensational costumes. Prior to her opening performance with *La revue nègre* at the Folies, Baker held bowls of cracked ice against her breasts to make them firm and pointed. Her trademark costume consisted simply of a skimpy

The can-can spectacular under the illuminated Eiffel Tower at the Folies Bergéres. (French Government Tourist Office.)

girdle of rhinestone-studded bananas in which the bare-breasted Baker enthusiastically danced the Charleston while her wildly moving body was reflected a thousand times as she moved before a background of mirrors. The audience applauded thunderously, and overnight Baker became the sensational reigning queen of the Folies.

Baker often referred to her long-legged body as being like a grasshopper's. Picasso sketched her, and Alexander Calder fashioned a wire sculpture of her dance pose. At the end of fifty years in French show business, a musical review of Baker's life was staged in which she sang more than thirty songs and danced vigorously. Only five days after this artistic triumph, in April 1975, she died in Paris.

11. Palace Théâtre
8, rue du Faubourg-Montmartre

The Dolly Sisters, an American music-hall act, were to appear in 1926 in a revue at another Paris theater with the famous French singer Mistinguett. But when the sisters found their names on the billboards in small letters while the French entertainer's was in massive print, they refused to appear and won a lawsuit against the management. Instead, the sisters played the Palace and headed the bill.

12. Residence of Jules Verne
18, boulevard Poissonnière

The French novelist and father of modern science fiction wrote *The Tour of the World in Eighty Days* while living here in 1873. Few people who saw *Around the World in Eighty Days,* the movie made from Verne's story, will forget the beauty of the scenery or the joy of the characters. Writers have noted that Verne was a frequent visitor to the nearby rue d'Amboise, famous for its many *maisons de joie* ("houses of joy"; brothels).

13. La Porte Montmartre
29, boulevard Poissonnière

In *Of Time and the River* (1935), Thomas Wolfe describes a night person sitting at this all-night café on the boulevard just opposite the rue du Faubourg-Montmartre and watching daylight spread across the sky behind Montmartre hill. "At first a wide strip of blue-grey—a strip of violet light. You see the line of the two clear and sharp." Then, Paris came alive.

14. Théâtre des Variétés
7, boulevard Montmartre

An oil painting by Jean Béraud in the Musée Carnavalet depicts the busy boulevard in front of the two-story façade of the theater. Blazing lights in the foyer illuminate the faces of the moving throng in the foreground. It is a true picture of the early-morning activity of the restaurants, brasseries, cafés, and theaters in this nocturnal area of Paris. Few artists lived in this area, but many frequented the busy streets.

15. Formerly Académie Julian
11–13, boulevard Montmartre, passage des Panoramas

Fifty glass-covered passages were built in Paris in the first half of the nineteenth century; these were the world's first shopping centers. American shipowner William Thayer constructed this passage and hired Robert Fulton to design the huge decorative panorama. (Later, when Fulton could not interest the French government in his steamboat, he returned to the United States).

This first teaching studio of Rodolphe Julian, founder of the Académie Julian, was opened in a former dance studio in 1868. The classes were attended by many French painters, including Bonnard, Vuillard, Matisse, Derain, and Léger. Julian ran the day-to-day activities, and celebrated artists of the time acted as tutors as they made weekly visits to criticize students' work.

According to Englishman George Moore:

In the studio were some 18 or 20 young men. . . . We sat around and drew from the model. . . . At 4 o'clock there was a general exodus from the studio; we adjourned to the neighboring café to drink beer.

Walk through the charming passage of small shops and cafés to just about the center where the galerie des Variétés crosses, then turn right to the exit onto rue Vivienne.

16. Formerly Académie Julian
51, rue Vivienne

The aspiring women artists were taught separately in a studio directed by Mme Julian, but the tutors were all men. Since the students drew from live nude models, this is probably the reason the men and women were separated. These were Victorian times.

17. Opéra-Comique
Rue Favart, place Boieldieu

When the playhouse was constructed in 1898, J. J. Benjamin-Constant decorated the ceiling with bright baroque images. Two years later, the young American soprano Mary Garden filled in for the French diva who suddenly became ill at the end of the second act of *Louise* by Gustave Charpentier. The French reviewers hailed Garden's performance and she sang the role for the next hundred productions. For her début she was paid 250 francs a month. By the time she returned to New York's Manhattan Opera Company in 1907, she was earning the handsome sum of 7,500 francs monthly. In 1926, she returned to Paris from Chicago to sing a farewell performance of the opera.

Cross over boulevard Haussmann. Now join Henry Miller and go "into the rue Laffitte which is just wide enough to frame the little

temple at the end of the street and above it the Sacré-Coeur, a kind
of exotic jumble of architecture."

18. Offices of *La revue blanche*
1, rue Laffitte

For fourteen years after Thadée Natanson and his brother
Alfred founded it in 1889, the weekly magazine *Revue blanche*
made lively reading, often treating important subjects with serious
insight. The Natansons and colleagues, writers Marcel Proust, Leo
Tolstoy, Anton Chekhov, Oscar Wilde, Mark Twain, Léon Blum (the
future premier of France), and painters Maurice Denis and Edouard
Vuillard, examined such topical subjects as population control,
women's place in society, socialism, and the plight of the worker.
The magazine offices were also used as exhibition space for the
works of artists unable to show in more traditional galleries.

*Henri Toulouse-Lautrec's poster of Misia for La revue
blanche. (Toulouse-Lautrec Musée d'Albi.)*

19. Gallery of Clovis Sagot
Rue Laffitte

Sagot was a clown turned art dealer whose gallery here sold Gertrude and Leo Stein their first Picasso painting. According to Gertrude's recollections, she did not like *Jeune fille aux fleurs* (*Young Girl with a Basket of Flowers*) because there was something "rather appalling about the drawing of the legs and feet of the nude little nymphet, standing in an Egyptian profile, her head turned, holding a basket of red flowers." The brother and sister argued over the merits of the Picasso work; he wanted to purchase it and she did not want it in the house. The next day at dinner, when he told her he had bought the disputed art piece, Gertrude threw down her knife and fork, exclaiming, "Now you've spoiled my appetite! I hated that picture with the feet like a monkey's." The purchase of the painting and the subsequent meeting of the American writer and the Spanish painter began a forty-one-year friendship, occasionally interrupted by disputes between these two eccentrics with sensitive egos.

20. Couture house of Callot Soeurs
24, rue Taitbout

This house of haute couture was founded in 1895 by three Callot sisters who loved to use delicate laces, gilt brocades, and gold fabrics on their turn-of-the-century creations. Their fine sewing and perfection of detail on day clothes, including matching parasols, and lingerie made from antique fabrics and fine delicate laces often copied exotic oriental designs.

21. Residence of Gustave Flaubert
(9), rue du Helder

In 1857, while living in the building that stood here, the French novelist wrote *Madame Bovary*. Like many authors, Flaubert admired composers, many of whom also wrote prose, and considered music a universal language. With few exceptions, such as the twentieth-century authors Ezra Pound and Jean Cocteau, writers did not compose music. On the morning of the première of Jules Massenet's *Le roi de Lahore* at the Paris Opéra on 27 April 1877, Flaubert left a card for Massenet which said: "This morning I pity you; tonight I shall envy you."

22. Le Grand Café Capucines
4, boulevard des Capucines

This elaborate nineteenth-century café should be visited in the evening when the colored-glass panels reflect the brilliantly lit interior. It is easy to imagine Oscar Wilde in one of his favorite haunts, seated here in the early morning hours. The café is still open round the clock every day.

23. Residence of Jacques Offenbach
8, boulevard des Capucines

As a young boy, Offenbach was brought here from Germany to study music; he stayed for the rest of his life. It was here, in 1876, that he composed the opera *Tales of Hoffman;* and when he invited his financial backers to a performance in the salon three years later, his four daughters and friends sang the principal roles. He died here 10 May 1880, almost a year before the opera was premièred.

24. Théâtre Nationale de l'Opéra
Place de l'Opéra

When the ornate palace of culture (named the Palais Garnier after the architect Jean Garnier) opened in 1875, it was the world's largest theater, with an area of nearly three acres and a stage large enough to hold 450 performers. Until 1989, the Paris Opéra and ballet performed in the opulent auditorium, but on 14 July 1989 the Bastille Opéra was inaugurated in celebration of the 200th anniversary of the French Republic. Now, only dance performances are staged here, but it is well worth the price of the ticket to see the six-ton chandelier hanging from a ceiling decorated by Marc Chagall in 1964 and the crimson brocade walls, walnut wood panelling, and gold curtain. Warning! Do not purchase the seats labeled "sans vue"; they really are without a view of the stage.

Nothing can compare in grandeur to the Grand Staircase sweeping upward to the Grand Foyer, about which Henry James wrote: "If the world were reduced to the domain of a single gorgeous potentate, the foyer would do very well for his throne room." The massive chamber, decorated in mirrors and allegorical paintings, is encrusted with gilt ornamentation.

On 29 May 1928, the European première of George Gershwin's Piano Concerto in F (with Vladimir Golschman conducting the orchestra and piano soloist Dimitri Tiomkin) was very well received

In front of the Paris Opera, 1900. (Bibliothèque de l'Opéra.)

by the audience. French critic Emile Vuillermoz wrote: "This very characteristic work made even the most distrustful musicians realize that . . . jazz might perfectly well exert a deep and beneficent influence in the most exalted spheres."

25. Le Café de la Paix
12, boulevard des Capucines

It is said that if you linger long enough on the terrace of the café, someone you know will walk by. While strolling by in the 1920s, American author Kay Boyle recognized friends sitting at a table. With them was Ernest Walsh. The next year, after a wet and freezing winter on the Normandy coast, a very ill Boyle, weak with lung disease, was invited by Walsh, a victim of tuberculosis, to join him in the Mediterranean town of Grasse. The thousand francs he sent her was to be an advance payment for her novel *Plagued by the Nightingale* (1931), which he planned to serialize in his magazine, *This Quarter*. Boyle, Walsh, and his wife and co-editor, Ethel Moorhead, established a ménage à trois in a stately, wisteria-clad villa. Soon Moorhead moved to Monte Carlo, leaving the two lovers to spend just six more months together. Ernest died in Monte Carlo in 1926 at the age of thirty-one, and his daughter by Boyle was born there six months later.

26. Formerly *Paris Herald*
49, avenue de l'Opéra

James Gordon Bennett, Jr., founded the European edition of the New York *Herald Tribune* on 4 October 1887. A crack yachtsman (he was always referred to as Commodore), Bennett introduced polo to the United States and was the son of the owner of the New York paper.

During the roaring twenties, when scores of Americans descended on Paris, the *Herald* became the paper of the "lobster palace Americans"—the Right Bank expatriates. A young Eric Sevareid was one of the latter-day distinguished journalists who wrote for the newspaper, along with William L. Shirer who, in his memoirs, called it "that rather absurd little house organ for the diminishing American colony." On 12 June 1940, just two days before the German army occupied Paris, the *Herald* stopped its presses, the last newspaper to discontinue publication. Those still in Paris especially missed the large reading room that had been open free to the public.

27. Formerly Le Café de Paris
41, avenue de l'Opéra

The cafés on the Grands Boulevards were some of the most famous in Paris and were frequented by many of the noted writers and artists of the late nineteenth century.

Up a flight of stairs, in the main dining rooms of the Café de Paris, Honoré de Balzac and Alexandre Dumas frequently enjoyed casseroled veal which, they claimed, could not fully be appreciated anywhere else. The ornate café closed in 1934, but a re-creation of the rooms is on view at the Musée Carnavalet.

28. Formerly Hôtel Bellevue
39, avenue de l'Opéra

In July 1880, while on his way to Glasgow, Scotland, to become the American consul, Bret Harte stayed here for a few days. He was already famous in America for his short stories "The Luck of Roaring Camp" and "The Outcasts of Poker Flat." He would become a popular figure in Great Britain, where he died in 1902.

After passing Brentano's, the bookseller that was established here nearly a hundred years ago, cross to the other side of the street.

29. Site of Impressionist Exhibition
28, avenue de l'Opéra

Fifteen artists participated in the fourth independent impressionist exhibition held here in 1879. Among the works shown were Degas's *Singer with Glove* and Caillebotte's *Rower in Top Hat,* but the big hit of the show was Renoir. That year he had painted an oil portrait of Alfred Sisley, a fellow student at Gleyre's studio who encouraged Renoir to become a pure impressionist.

Walk toward the Opéra and turn right at rue Gaillon.

30. Restaurant Drouant
18, place Gaillon

In *Of Time and the River,* Thomas Wolfe describes a meal at the Drouant that cost less than $2: consommé, rump steak, fonds d'artichaut Mornay, coffee, and half a bottle of Nuits Saint-Georges wine.

When the Anglo-American Press Association of Paris met at a weekly lunch in 1939, Waverly Root and A. J. Liebling, both newspapermen and gourmands, met for the first time. Liebling described Root:

A kindly and humorous man of wide and disparate interests, he could talk well of many things, but our conversations, from the day I met him, were preponderantly about what we had eaten, or were about to eat or wished to eat.

Cross the small square and go one short block, then turn left.

31. Couture house of Paul Poiret
22, rue d'Antin

Poiret worked as a designer for the houses of Doucet (1897–1900) and Worth (1901–1904) before opening his own couture business in 1904; then in 1909 he relocated here. The first of the fashion celebrity designers so highly publicized today, Poiret had a personality as renowned as his designs. He was the earliest couturier to believe that a dress could be a work of art and to view the artists of his day as his colleagues.

For six years, until he left for the frontline trenches in 1914 dressed in a uniform of his own design, Poiret's spectacular designs freed women from the hourglass silhouette and the Belle Epoque's overdone profusion of colors and fabrics. The Poiret woman was slender in her long straight dress of primary colors and simple decorations; gone were the corsets and ruffled petticoats.

After the end of the war, Poiret reopened his design house, but now he had real competition. Other designers were showing simple costumes, stressing the art and skill of fine dressmaking. Poiret's designs looked theatrical from a distance but, unfortunately, when examined closely, were poorly constructed.

32. Office of William Bird
19, rue d'Antin

This was the headquarters of the Consolidated Press Association of Washington, D.C., in 1920 when William Bird was the European manager. The next year he established the Three Mountains Press in a former wine cellar on the Ile Saint-Louis. While attending the Genoa Economic Conference in Italy, the tall, thin, academic-looking Bird met fellow reporter Ernest Hemingway. It was Hemingway who recommended Ezra Pound and his work to Bird, who later appointed Pound editor of the small press. Ford Madox Ford's novel *Women and Men* (1923) was chosen by Pound to be included in the first edition of six books.

Ford was the editor of *Transatlantic Review,* a new English-language magazine with offices in the same building. The unpaid assistant editor was the young Ernest Hemingway, whose book *In Our Time* Bird published in 1924.

33. Formerly Hôtel d'Orient
6, rue Daunou

Fifty years after he completed his medical studies in Paris, Oliver Wendell Holmes, Sr., returned in August 1886 to stay here. While in Paris, Holmes visited only one person, Louis Pasteur, who the previous year had completed the technique of vaccination against anthrax, which also protects against rabies. Describing the visit in *One Hundred Days in Europe* (1887), Holmes noted:

> I told him I was an American physician who wished to look in his face and take his hand. . . . I looked in his face, which was that of a thoughtful, hard-working student. . . . I took his hand, which has performed some of the most delicate and daring experiments ever ventured upon.

34. Harry's New York Bar
5, rue Daunou

When the bar opened on Thanksgiving Day 1911, the Opéra

district was the commercial and social center of Paris. This has always been a neighborhood of banks, but then there were many more permanent residents in the surrounding hotels and the grand apartments. A Mr. Clancy dismantled the New York Bar in New York City and shipped the counter and mahogany wood panelling to Paris, where he went into business with the popular jockey Tod Sloane. Harry McElhone, a Scot from Dundee, was behind the bar on opening day and, in 1924, he became the owner of the first Harry's Bar. Today his son Andrew and grandson Duncan manage the venerable establishment. Stories abound about Americans in Europe who hung out here, including F. Scott Fitzgerald, Ernest Hemingway, and the Dolly Sisters. Did George Gershwin really compose parts of *An American in Paris* on the Downstairs Room piano?

On one of my visits, Andy told me that in 1936 surrealist artist Hiller Hilaire was experimenting with painting on blankets by first applying oil paint, then setting the design with a hot iron. Because

Harry McElhone at the 1911 opening of Harry's New York Bar. (Courtesy of Duncan McElhone.)

the project involved such hard work, he only created a few, one of which was donated to Harry.

When the German army occupied Paris in 1940, the bar was kept open and run by the French as an enemy property business. The cellars were bare in 1944, a few days after the liberation, upon Harry's return from England to greet his friends, including Hemingway, as they returned to Paris. Today Americans and French citizens order Bloody Marys, Side Cars, and White Ladys, drinks that originated and were first served at Harry's. This is a good place to complete your stroll with a hot dog, introduced in France by Harry in 1925 and still cooked in an antique steamer.

From here it is an easy stroll back to the Métro Opéra.

SCENE

DESIGNS
FOR THE
RITZ

FIVE

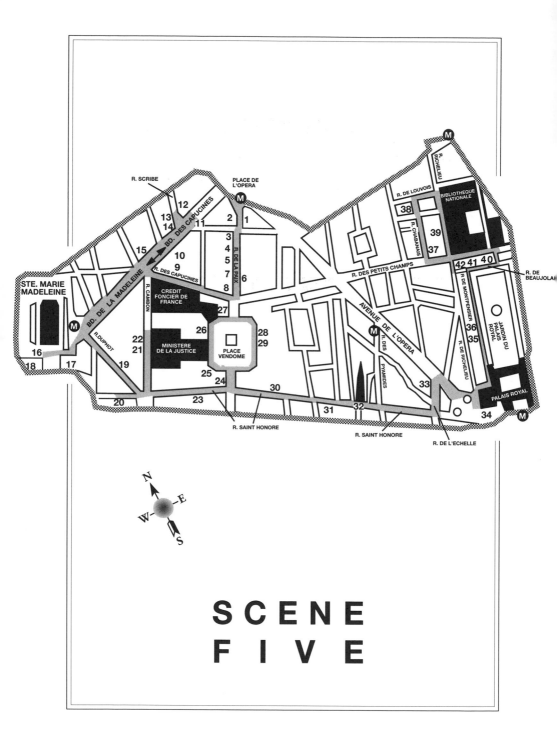

SCENE
FIVE

Is fashion art? Some critics say no because it is utilitarian. If that is true, what about Picasso's functional ceramic plates and bowls, Louis XIV furniture, and Giacometti's benches and tables in the Musée Picasso? The traditional definition of art has changed. In the twentieth-century Musée d'Orsay, architecture, furnishings, film, and crafts are viewed as art; the De Young Museum in San Francisco and the Brooklyn Museum in New York have recently presented costume exhibitions. Jean Dreusedow of the Metropolitan Museum's Costume Institute states: "Fashion is not just clothes, especially with haute couture. High fashion is always part of the aesthetic context of its time." Clothes mirror the society and decade in which they are produced.

The history of haute couture begins on the rue de la Paix in the nineteenth century when the nouveaux riches of the industrial revolution desired to flaunt their financial position. For the first time, people didn't need to inherit status; they could purchase the advice of an art dealer, hire an architect to build a mansion in the right part of town, and engage a fashionable couturier to provide a correct wardrobe. The modish person reflected the taste of the expert.

Pioneer French designers Worth, Poiret, Paquin, and Lanvin were responsible for the present-day description of a designer-dressmaker: an artist whose craft and taste is reflected in everything he creates.

This stroll includes the venerable Hôtel Ritz. On the eve of World War I, a stylish society woman dining at the hotel with Marcel Proust would have listened to the poet Léon-Paul Fargue recite:

What do rich girls dream about?
The hotel life.
Which hotels do they like best?
They all like the same one best: the Ritz.
What is the Ritz?
It's Paris.
And what is Paris?
The Ritz.

Métro Opéra
Buses 42, 20

The place de l'Opéra is a frenetic area. Exit the busy station and head south in the direction of the Seine. I find it easier to orient myself in central Paris if I use the river as my mark: I am going toward, away from, upstream, or downstream.

1. Short-term residence of Henry James
20, rue de la Paix, formerly Hôtel de Hollande

Step inside the front door where you can see the original entrance of the elegant hotel. On 24 October 1889, Henry James took a room and stayed for two months. During this time he visited the Universal Exhibition and completed writing *The Tragic Muse* (1890). In an evening meeting with Alphonse Daudet, he agreed to translate the French author's latest Tartarin novel.

2. Couture house of Jacques Doucet
17 and 21, rue de la Paix

For fifty years Doucet's grandmother maintained a shop selling fine laces at number 17; in 1869 the shop was divided into two adjoining shops: a shirtmaker for men and lace and lace-trimmed lingerie for women at number 17, and at number 21 Jacques Doucet established his maison de couture in 1871.

The third generation of the Doucet family to sell women's furnishings, Jacques loved elegance and set himself as the arbiter of good taste in both his professional and private life. He built a reputation as a connoisseur of eighteenth-century artworks and paintings, then collected and supported the impressionists and avant-garde artists. It was Doucet who purchased Picasso's 1907 revolutionary cubist painting *Les demoiselles d'Avignon* (*The Women of Avignon*) in 1909, then built a special wing in his house for it to hang at the top of a crystal staircase.

The clientèle of the House of Doucet were dressed in dignity and luxury that reflected the elegance displayed in eighteenth-century French paintings. For his good taste, Doucet was praised by Proust in *Remembrances of Things Past* (1913–27), but he never adapted to the simplicity and ease of the post–World War I fashion world. After his death in 1929, the house closed; he had dressed one generation of women but never really attracted the loyalty of their daughters. The shop selling gentlemen's accoutrements is still in business at number 21, rue de la Paix.

3. Short-term residence of Henry James
13, rue de la Paix, Hôtel Westminster

Twelve-year-old Henry James, brother William, and their

parents stayed here in June 1856 while searching for a permanent residence for a year in Paris. The experience in France had a consequential influence on the young Henry, who later wrote that France was "the mysterious home of art, the country who had given her inhabitants something called Taste, which distinguished them from other people."

4. Couture house of Boué Soeurs
9, rue de la Paix

Sisters Sylvie and Jeanne Boué established their dressmaking house in 1899. Their distinctive lingerie and daytime dresses of sheer fabrics and fine silks were ornamented by embroidery made in Venice and silver and gold lace from their workrooms.

It was easy to recognize their clothing: it had the look of lingerie in delicate pastel colors and was trimmed in lace and adorned with their signature silk ribbon rosettes. When the French sisters opened the first couture house in New York, their designs were more popular in America than in Europe. By 1933 the business had closed.

5. Couture house of Charles Frederick Worth
7, rue de la Paix

Englishman Charles Frederick Worth is probably most famous for changing the entire way in which clothing had been produced until the mid-1880s. Until Worth, female dressmakers dressed specific royal figures; the feminine word *couturière* was adapted from the masculine *couturier* when Worth became the first man to design and produce fashionable clothes for the members of the court of Empress Eugénie. As he was the first to sign his name (along with an embroidered royal crest) to his creations, Worth invented the designer label now prevalent on everything from clothes to sheets.

Beginning as a men's tailor in 1845, five years later he started to design outfits for his wife. Then, in 1858, Marie and Charles Worth formed a partnership with Otto Bobergh, and the house of Worth and Bobergh was born at this address. The name Worth stood alone in bold block letters when, in 1871, Bobergh returned to Sweden.

Until the business moved in 1936, wealthy worldly women with social ambitions included a stop here to order original creations; the international reputation was gained because of the high

Clothing designer Charles Frederick Worth. (Bibliothèque Nationale.)

quality of the garments and the status they conferred on the wearer. At one time, Worth dressed most of the crowned heads of Europe as well as American socialites such as Consuelo Vanderbilt, Mrs. J. Pierpont Morgan, and Mrs. William Astor. Worth preferred American clients to European royalty: queens asked the price; Americans asked only that they be shown the finest.

6. Couture house of Elsa Schiaparelli
4, rue de la Paix

While Worth dressed women in courtly tasteful luxury, Schiaparelli's career was built on shockingly revolutionary creations in bold new colors. The Spanish designer Balenciaga contrasted the two leading female French couturières of the 1930s: "Coco [Chanel] had very little taste, but it was very good. Schiap, on the other hand, had lots of it, but it was bad."

Born in Italy in 1896, the thirty-year-old Elsa made her bow into the Paris fashion world in 1928 with a black-and-white wool pullover sweater. She rented a studio on an upper floor here and for the next two years produced innovative sportswear. In 1930, she moved to a street-level shop and added evening dresses and costumes "for the city" in unusual fabrics, then included the accessories, jewelry, hats, and belts.

In one of the few successful collaborations between artists and couturiers, Salvador Dali, Jean Cocteau, and Louis Aragon designed for Schiaparelli; Dali painted a lobster on an evening dress and garnished it with sprigs of parsley, and poet Aragon devised a necklace of what looked like a string of aspirins. The author Caroline Milbank wrote:

> *Just as the Dadaists mocked the notion of good art, Schiaparelli mocked the notion of good taste, knowing that as women became increasingly confident, rules about propriety and taste could be more effective if broken.*

7. Couture house of M. and Mme Paquin
3, rue de la Paix

From its founding in 1890 through the 1920s, the design house of Paquin was famous for its originality and opulence. Mme Paquin was the designer, while her husband, who had financed the business with profits from the French stock market, served as administrator. They were the first of the couture houses to open branches outside of Paris.

Perhaps Madame was best known for her fur-trimmed coats and her insistence that the clothes move with the woman for, as she once wrote, while designing she kept in her thoughts "those Parisiennes who must battle with the Métro."

Jean Béraud, The Worker's Entrance at the House of Paquin, *about 1902. (Musées de la Ville de Paris.)*

8. Formerly design house of Grès
1, rue de la Paix

On the first and second floors, look for the signs that denote the former workrooms of the house of Grès. In 1942, during the German occupation of Paris, the house of Grès relocated to this spot. Since 1934, Mme Grès had concentrated on designing clothes for a select clientèle, refusing to be influenced by fads or what the average woman would wear. The classic designs are so timeless that many owners today are proud of wearing a vintage original Grès creation.

Turn right at the corner.

9. Couture house of Nina Ricci
20, rue des Capucines

In collaboration with her son Robert, head of the business today, Mme Ricci founded her fashion house here in 1932. Operating out of a single room, Nina created the fashions and Robert ran and promoted the business. The couture house grew rapidly in the thirties, and at the start of World War II it occupied eleven floors in three buildings. Mme Ricci described her design goals thus:

To achieve the maximum lightness so that the dress would be perfect for dancing; to give the dress a lot of quietness that, in her mind, would render it most appealing to the youthful; and to find just that elegant detail that would make the dress be a client's favorite.

Turn right again onto the boulevard.

10. Studio of Félix Nadar
35, boulevard des Capucines

Photographer Nadar's old studio at this location is more famous as the site of the first exhibition by the group of painters known as the impressionists than as the place where Nadar lived and worked. In April and May 1874, the cooperative Société anonyme des artistes, peintres, sculpteurs, graveurs, etc. presented a show organized by Pissarro, Monet, Renoir, and Degas; it was not sanctioned by the French government or juried. The avant-garde show was of extreme importance because it laid the foundation for the modernist revolution in all segments of the world of art.

The impressionists were loathed by the critics and by the traditional artists of the beaux-arts school such as art teacher Pierre Guichard, who wrote to the mother of Berthe Morisot upon viewing Morisot's work in the show:

One does not associate with madmen except at some peril. . . . All the exhibitors are a bit touched in the head. If Mlle Berthe is set on doing something violent she should pour petrol on these things and set them alight rather than destroy all she has done so far.

11. Short-term residence of Oscar Wilde
29, boulevard des Capucines

Late in 1891, Wilde stayed in the hotel here while writing the controversial play *Salomé*. Russian dancer Ida Rubenstein staged the play in December 1908 to the music of Glazunov, and in the "Dance of the Seven Veils" she removed the veils one by one until she appeared totally nude. The Russian Orthodox church had censored the performance, but she received their permission to stage the work by promising not to speak Wilde's original lines. To the delight of a wildly enthusiastic audience, she performed silently in mime.

12. Banquet for Sarah Bernhardt
2, rue Scribe, Le Grand Hôtel

One of Europe's oldest luxury hotels, the six-hundred-room Grand was designed by Charles Garnier, the designer of the nearby Paris Opéra.

At noon on 9 December 1896, five hundred admirers attended a banquet here for Sarah Bernhardt. Making her theatrical entrance in a magnificent, gold-embroidered white dress trimmed in chinchilla, a long train of English lace sweeping behind, Bernhardt descended a curved staircase in an incomparable series of poses that brought the hushed audience to its feet. As the guests raised their glasses to the "Divine Sarah," bravos rang out.

13. Short-term residence of John Dos Passos
1, rue Scribe, Hôtel Scribe

When John Dos Passos stayed at the Hôtel Scribe as a war correspondent at the close of World War II, he was returning to the Paris he had lived in after serving as a Red Cross ambulance driver in World War I and then as a roving newspaper correspondent. In 1945, at the age of forty-nine, his early enthusiasm for France was dampened by the visible scars of the suffering of war: "Life was not the same—it was drearier and deadlier."

Turn right, back onto the boulevard.

14. Cinema of Louis and Auguste Lumière
14, boulevard des Capucines

In what was called the Salon Indien, on 28 December 1895, the Lumière brothers showed to the public cinematic photographs of Paris views that were the inaugural moving pictures. During the projection some of the audience were terrified that the two moving trains pulling into the Ciotat station would run over them.

15. Ballet school of Zelda Fitzgerald
28, boulevard des Capucines, Olympia Music Hall

Mme Lubov Egorova, director of the ballet school for the Diaghilev Ballets Russes, maintained a studio above the theater. Zelda and F. Scott Fitzgerald were spending the summer of 1928 in Paris and, at the age of twenty-eight, Zelda was determined to become a ballerina. Their good friend Gerald Murphy arranged for instruction from Mme Egorova, once a leading ballerina with

Diaghilev's troop and now a superb coach. Zelda worked feverishly for more than eight hours a day in what she later wrote was her desire to find something of her own that would separate her from Scott. The stage of the rehearsal room was built on a slope that was two feet higher on one end, giving the audience a view of the dancer the entire time. Murphy described his visit to watch Zelda perform:

There was something dreadfully grotesque in her intensity— one could see the muscles individually stretch and pull; her legs looked muscular and ugly. It was really terrible. . . . Thank God, she couldn't see what she looked like. When I watched Zelda that afternoon in Paris, I thought to myself, she's going to try and hold on to her youth. You know, there's nothing worse. It ruins a woman.

16. Funeral of Josephine Baker
Place de la Madeleine, Eglise Sainte-Marie-Madeleine

Fifty-two huge Corinthian pillars rise at the top of the twenty-eight steps leading to the church, which was consecrated in 1842. Grand funerals have been held here, including Frédéric Chopin's in 1849, at which his composition "Funeral March" was given its première performance on the magnificent organ.

The greatest and most elegant funeral was that of Josephine Baker on 15 April 1975. Scores of open trucks held the hundreds of flower displays that were later placed on the monuments to those who died in World War II. For the first time, the French honored an American woman with a twenty-one-gun salute. For fifty years the French adored her, copied her, and talked about her. Her theme song, "J'ai deux amours" ("I have two loves, my country and Paris"), was never to be sung again in France.

17. Formerly Restaurant Durand
2, place de la Madeleine

Emile Zola, an ardent social reformer, sat in this restaurant in 1898 while writing *J'accuse*. It was his bitter indictment of the French establishment's handling of the Dreyfus affair (the entrapment and persecution of a Jewish French officer by antisemitic fellow officers). When Zola was prosecuted for libel because of the book, he fled to England.

18. Residence of Jean Cocteau
9, place de la Madeleine

Cocteau, who lived in an apartment in this building, was described as "the frivolous prince," the title of a book of poems he published at the age of twenty-one. He walked with a swagger, dressed fashionably and elegantly, always had a fresh gardenia in his buttonhole (he was rumored to have received the flower daily from London), and gossiped in a mocking, irreverent manner. André Gide describes meeting Cocteau for tea in 1914:

I did not enjoy seeing him again even though he made himself extremely agreeable; he simply cannot be serious and to me all his aphorisms, his witticisms, his reactions, and the extraordinary brio [vigor] of his customary way of talking were as shocking as a luxury article on display in a period of famine and mourning.

19. Short-term residence of Thomas Wolfe
8, rue Duphot, Hôtel Burgundy

For a few weeks in July 1927, Thomas Wolfe stayed here while working on the last section of his large, somewhat autobiographical novel, *Look Homeward, Angel* (1929). The fictionalized story was completed in March 1928, after just twenty months of intense writing. Only four days later, in what turned out to be a good decision, he resigned his teaching position at New York University to become a full-time professional writer.

Turn right at the end of the street.

20. Possible birthplace of Sarah Bernhardt
(265), rue Saint-Honoré

The exact address of the great French tragédienne's birthplace in Paris on 23 October 1844 is disputed; the building formerly on this site is one that is listed. Bernhardt's father was supposedly a Belgian student unmarried to Judith Van Hard, an exceptionally beautiful *demimondaine* (courtesan) whose life-style did not include a child. Until the age of four the baby was raised by a nurse in Brittany, then by her mother's sister Rosine. For the next four years Sarah lived here with her mother in a chic flat, but was not taught to read or write until the age of eight, when she was sent to Mme Fressard's boarding school for young ladies. Judith, now Youle, visited her young daughter only twice during the next two years. Although from a staunch Dutch Jewish middle-class family, Youle enrolled Sarah at the age of ten in a convent at Versailles, because the Parisian smart set was Catholic and she had plans for a future good marriage for her neglected daughter.

Backtrack and turn left on rue Cambon.

21. Residence of James
29, rue Cambon

At the age of thirty-two, in 1875, James rented a third-floor apartment here consisting of a parlor, two bedrooms, a dining room, and a kitchen, all for the sum of $65 a month. As James later wrote to a friend:

> I am turning into an old, and very contented, Parisian: I feel as if I had stuck roots into the Parisian soil. . . . It is a very comfortable and profitable place. . . . The great merit of the place is that one can arrange one's life here exactly as one pleases—that there are facilities for every kind of habit and taste, and that everything is accepted and understood.

James was ahead of his time; in the early part of the twentieth century, the American expatriates claimed the freedom Paris offered the individual was the reason they were attracted to the city.

James had been hired to write a weekly letter, "Paris through Fresh Eyes," for the New York *Tribune*. After twenty letters, for $20 each, the letters ceased because, he wrote to his mother, "subjects were woefully scarce."

22. Couture house of Coco Chanel
31, rue Cambon

At number 21, in 1910, the plaque on the door read "Chanel Modes." Upstairs, Mlle Chanel created hats in a business financed by her paramour "Boy" Capel. Within a few years, when she was filling orders for dresses to match the hats, the designs brought women's fashions into the twentieth century, free from stiff fabrics, layers of petticoats, uncomfortable shoes, and elaborate hairdos. Women now had the option of being both comfortable and stylish. In response to her own need for comfort at the seaside resorts, Chanel invented sportswear—flannel blazers, men's trousers, long jersey sweaters, and sailor tops. A modern woman could appear at the smart resort Deauville today dressed in a timeless Chanel outfit and look and feel appropriately outfitted.

The private apartment of Coco Chanel. (Courtesy of Chanel, Paris.)

By 1920 the House of Chanel had expanded to number 31.

The grand salon reflects the deceptive simplicity of Chanel's designs for little black dresses, jersey dresses, suits, and costume jewelry. The large beige room with plain art-deco-style modern chandeliers has many reflecting mirrors, creating the impression of endless space. Up a grand mirror-lined curving staircase, from which Chanel often watched the presentation of her latest collection, is her lavish second-floor private apartment. The walls of the three rooms are papered in copper-gold, the floors are covered by priceless antique oriental carpets, and the furnishings demonstrate Chanel's use of beige, black, and gold. The relatively small rooms contain large pieces, including priceless laquered Coromandel screens, and a library of signed first-edition books. She did not sleep here at night. When the weather was stormy she wore boots for her short walk across the street to the rear entrance of the Hôtel Ritz so she could spend the night in her small room, where she died in 1971.

Christian Dior said of Chanel: "With a black sweater and ten rows of pearls, [she] revolutionized fashion." Her influence went beyond clothes, jewelry, and perfume; many houses all over the world show her influence. She virtually invented the use of the color beige and liked the colors black, white, gold, and red for clothes and furnishings, as well as natural-colored wood. In the small rooms of her private apartment, she was the first to use large pieces of furniture and enormous mirrors to give the little rooms a perspective of openness. "Some people think luxury is the contrary of being poor," Chanel once said in her crisp manner. "It is not. It is the contrary of vulgarity." Her influence went beyond her work to a new way of living and being in the twentieth century, for, as she stated, "Fashion passes, style remains."

Retrace your steps back to rue Saint-Honoré and turn left.

23. Summer residence of Cornelia Otis Skinner
239, rue Saint-Honoré, Hôtel de France et Choiseul

This former convent was home to the auspicious actor Otis Skinner and his family in the summers of 1920 and 1921. His daughter Cornelia Otis later wrote *Madame Sarah* (1966), a biography of Sarah Bernhardt. When Cornelia asked her father if he considered Bernhardt to have been the greatest actress he ever saw, he answered: "I don't know, certainly she was the greatest show woman."

24. Vacation residence of Fred Astaire
1, place Vendôme, Hôtel Vendôme

Fred Astaire and his wife stayed at this small hotel in 1936 for privacy and anonymity. He had just completed *Swing Time* with Ginger Rogers and was vacationing and resting before starting the film *Shall We Dance?*

25. Residence of J. P. Morgan
3-5, place Vendôme, formerly Hôtel Bristol

From 1890 to 1910, John Pierpont Morgan, an uncle of dilettante publisher Harry Crosby, always occupied the same first-floor suite on his Paris visits. The hotel, owned by a former butler of Morgan's father, was besieged by art dealers when J. P. was in residence because he was an avid collector and president of the New York Metropolitan Museum.

26. A favorite hotel of Ernest Hemingway
15, place Vendôme, Hôtel Ritz

Ritz, synonymous with luxury and elegance, in the hotel industry means the Paris Ritz. César Ritz, the youngest child of a Swiss goatherder, established in 1898 the most opulent hotel in Paris—perhaps in the world.

During World War II, Mme Ritz and her son Charles managed the hotel under the direction of the German occupation government, which used it to billet such high Nazi officers as Marshal Hermann Goering. In June 1944 the Allied forces liberated Paris and Ernest Hemingway "liberated" the Ritz from the German occupiers, after first taking French bookshop owner Adrienne Monnier's last bar of soap to wash his shirts. Because the famous writer spent so much time in the Ritz Bar, it has been renamed the Hemingway Bar, with an entrance on the rue Cambon.

27. Couture house of Schiaparelli
21, place Vendôme

This is the address woven into the present Schiaparelli label because the business was moved here in 1934. The shop was closed for part of the Second World War and then reopened in 1945. Perfumes as well as ready-to-wear and boutique items can be purchased here.

28. The Obelisk Press
16, place Vendôme

In an office in the rear overlooking an interior courtyard of this building, English publisher Jack Kahane produced some very controversial books, many of them labeled as pornographic or obscene. After reading the manuscript of Henry Miller's *Tropic of Cancer,* written in Paris, Kahane exclaimed, "I had in my hands a work of genius and it had been offered to me for publication." When the book appeared in September 1934, the cover carried an admonition to booksellers that the book was not to be displayed in the window, but word of the book's contents and superb writing spread so quickly that in Paris, although some bookshops sold the book from under the counter, one store in Montparnasse discounted the warning and put the book in the window. On the jacket of the first edition appeared a quote by writer Anaïs Nin, a good friend of Miller's, that left little doubt of the book's contents:

*In a world grown paralyzed with introspection and consti-
pated by delicate mental meals this brutal exposure of the
substantial body comes as a vitalizing current of blood. The
violence and obscenity are left unadulterated, as manifesta-
tion of the mystery and pain which ever accompanies the act
of creation.*

29. Business address of Harry Crosby
14, place Vendôme, Morgan Harjes et Cie.

Boston socialite Harry Crosby was involved in a scandalous
love affair with the married Polly Peabody, so his mother, one of the
wealthy banking Morgans, shipped him off to Paris in 1922 for
employment in the French division of Morgan Guaranty Trust
Company. But neither Harry's family nor Polly's husband could
stop the inevitable: after Polly's divorce, they married and, accompanied by her son and daughter, settled in Paris.

Most of Crosby's banking hours were spent at the Ritz Bar or
the gambling tables. On 31 December of that same year he left his
desk at the bank forever; he believed, as Schopenhauer had written:
"Social rules are made by normal people for normal people, the man
of genius is fundamentally abnormal." Harry felt he was different
from the rest of society and hoped that through writing poetry he
could discover his genius. Until his suicide in 1929, the Crosbys'
Black Sun Press published their love poems to each other as well
as works by Archibald MacLeish, Marcel Proust, and Henry James.

30. Residence of Edouard Vuillard
342, rue Saint-Honoré

At the time the twenty-nine-year-old avant-garde Nabis painter
Vuillard wrote to his fellow artist Félix Vallotton from this address
in 1897, he described his ménage à trois with Misia and Thadée
Natanson. The threesome shared a country villa and frequently
travelled together. Fifty years later, Misia wrote of an encounter
with Vuillard: "Suddenly our eyes met. In the growing darkness I
could see only the gleam of his sad eyes. He burst into sobs. It was
the most beautiful declaration of love any man ever made to me."

31. Short-term residence of Sinclair Lewis
211, rue Saint-Honoré, Hôtel Saint-James et d'Albany

Sinclair Lewis had achieved fame as a novelist with the publication of *Main Street* (1920). When he stayed here with his wife and son in October 1921, he was writing *Babbitt* (1922), but Paris offered too many diversions, so he returned home and the book was published the next year; he did return to Paris in 1925.

32. Marriage site of Misia and José-María Sert
Rue Saint-Honoré and rue Saint-Roch, Eglise Saint-Roch

Forty-eight-year-old and twice-divorced Misia (Natanson) Edwards married Spanish artist José-María Sert in this church on 2 August 1920. They had lived together for the previous twelve years and the optimistic Sert said: "She is the only woman capable of understanding me and putting up with me."

33. Short-term residence of Mark Twain
7, rue de l'Echelle, Hôtel Normandy

"April in Paris" is a very romantic notion because it is usually raining. Mark Twain stayed in this hotel in the spring of 1879 while reviewing *A Tramp Abroad* (1879), rereading Thomas Carlyle's *History of the French Revolution,* and writing. On 7 May he wrote: "I wish this terrible winter would come to an end. Have had rain almost without intermission for two months and one week."

Cross the place Colette to the porticoed theater.

34. Comédie-Française
2, rue de Richelieu

On 6 November 1872, Sarah Bernhardt opened to a full house of sophisticated, chic, and critical theater patrons who noticed a difference between her performance in the early part of the play and the last act. In the initial scenes she appeared as a young actress inadequate for the part, and then in the final act the famous Bernhardt magic shone. Bernhardt explained this uneven performance by stating that shortly after the beginning of the play her mother suddenly rose in her stage box, obviously in great pain, and then staggered out. At the beginning of the last act, Bernhardt was signalled that, although her mother had suffered a heart attack, she was now all right.

35. Harrison of Paris Press
30, rue de Montpensier

Although the worldwide economic depression that began in 1929 drove most of the small English-language publications in Paris out of business, in 1930 Barbara Harrison financed a new quality press. Monroe Wheeler, a talented typographical designer and printer, supervised the production of exceedingly fine limited editions. In three years, they published twelve works, including the final version of Katherine Anne Porter's *Hacienda* (1934), and a collection of seven stories by Bret Harte, *The Wild West: Stories of Bret Harte* (1930), that included "The Outcasts of Poker Flat" and "The Luck of Roaring Camp." In publishing Harte's book, Harrison claimed her aim was to print a book worthy of the "good and handsome Californian."

36. Residence of Jean Cocteau
36, rue de Montpensier

Three arcaded sides of the Palais Royale contain elegant

Self-portrait by Jean Cocteau, 1948. (Bibliothèque Nationale.)

apartments that face on a large garden dotted with lime trees and lavish fountains. Philippe, Duke of Orléans, had the square constructed in 1780 and named the galleries and adjoining streets after his three sons: Valois, Beaujolais, and Montpensier.

Poet and dramatist Cocteau lived in one of the sought-after apartments. When Picasso, whom Cocteau described as "the great encounter" of his life, drew his portrait in an army-style uniform, Cocteau wrote to a friend: "This morning, I pose for Picasso in his studio. He is beginning an 'Ingres' head of me—very suitable for portrait of young author to accompany his works after premature death."

37. Formerly The Chabanois
12, rue Chabanois

Opened in 1878 for the Paris Exhibition, this famous bordello was reputed to have been the favorite maison de joie of the English Prince of Wales (King Edward VII). Included in the auction of its furnishings after World War II was one item described as the bathtub reserved exclusively for His Royal Highness.

This description of The Chabanois affords us a view of an upper-class Parisian brothel:

The salons are sumptuous, each one represents a cabin in a pleasure yacht, and with elegant bathrooms. Visitors are received in a magnificent hall modeled from a courtyard of the Spanish Alhambra and are given an illustrated booklet of views of the best apartments in the eight-storied house. Every flat is divided into numerous rooms, neatly furnished in correct Louis XV style.

38. Short-term residence of A. J. Liebling
1, rue Lulli, formerly Hôtel Louvois

Gourmand newsman A. J. Liebling stayed at the hotel in 1939 while assigned as a correspondent to cover the fast-developing war in Europe for *The New Yorker*. When he left for the war action in June 1940, with fellow food lover Chicago *Tribune* correspondent Waverly Root, only six guests remained in the 180-room hotel, with seven staff members.

39. Residence of Stendha
61, rue de Richelieu

Henri Beyle adopted the pseudonym of Stendhal and lived here in 1822–23. Liebling, describing a statue of the author, wrote that his large protruding front is "a magnificent background for a watchchain, an advantageous stuffing for a brocaded waistcoat." Most of Stendhal's contemporary French writers, except his friend Balzac, were antagonized by his spare prose and disdain for the lush romantic works then in vogue.

40. Residence of Sidonie-Gabrielle Colette
9, rue de Beaujolais

Ten years before their marriage in 1935, Colette, age fifty-three and author of the Claudine stories, and Maurice Goudeket, age thirty-six, moved into this apartment which Colette referred to as a "tunnel" because windows were only in the front and rear. But a French journalist described it as

> one of those delightful and irregular apartments which look over the former gardens of the Ducs d'Orléans. The ceiling is elliptical, like the lid of a box, and this doll's apartment is in fact a box lined with cretonne and full of superannuated and rococo which Colette collected long before the world took notice of them.

In a story published in Brinnon's book *Sextette* (1961), Truman Capote recalled:

> One day I went to see Colette, tea for two, in a boudoir that smelled of sachet and cat pissat. Cocteau had warned me she'd never heard of me. . . . The old darling, she looks like a doll saved from a fire.

The work of Colette is largely the study of feminine psychology. Her novels *Chérie* (1920) and *La fin de Chérie* (1926) detailed her own life story with its many love affairs. Perhaps Americans are most familiar with her story *Gigi* (1941), because it was dramatized for the stage by Anita Loos and then made into a movie starring Leslie Caron in the role of Gigi (Colette), a young schoolgirl in love with a handsome older man—Bertrand de Jouvenel in Colette's real life.

In August 1953, at the age of eighty, Colette died in the room where she had spent many hours propped up by pillows in front of a window overlooking the gardens, watching her old friends, the trees, and breathing in the people and their adventures. She was the first Frenchwoman to be given a state funeral and thousands passed before her tricouleur-draped coffin, placed in the court of honor of the Palais Royal. She had written her own epitaph: "Winter no more has an end than spring has a beginning, and the earth does not know either death or rest."

41. Short-term residence of Sylvia Beach and Margaret Anderson
15, rue de Beaujolais, formerly Hôtel Beaujolais

Sylvia Beach and her sister Cyprian met in Paris in 1917 and stayed in this former hotel frequented by actors and visiting Spaniards. The Palais Royal theater next door presented the naughtiest plays in Paris. Believing John Howard Payne had written "Home Sweet Home" at the Palais Royal, Sylvia wrote: "To think that his wistful ''Mid pleasures and palaces' had been written in such a shabby old palace."

After service in World War I with the American Red Cross, Sylvia returned to Paris in 1919 to study contemporary French literature at the Sorbonne. Adrienne Monnier, proprietor of a Left Bank bookshop, introduced Sylvia to her prominent friends, French writers André Gide, Paul Valéry, and Jules Romains. With Adrienne's encouragement and help, in late 1919 Beach established Shakespeare and Company, the most celebrated American bookshop in Europe and the Paris home to noted authors Ernest Hemingway, James Joyce, T. S. Eliot, and Ezra Pound.

Another American resident of the old hotel was Margaret Anderson, who moved to France in 1923. When Anderson published early excerpts of James Joyce's *Ulysses* (formally published by Shakespeare and Company in 1922), in 1918, 1919, and 1920 issues of her *Little Review,* the U.S. Post Office burned the July-August 1920 issues on grounds of obscenity. After a 1921 trial, Margaret and her partner Jane Heap were fined $50 each and instructed never to publish *Ulysses* again.

42. Le Grand Véfour
17, rue de Beaujolais

Walk into the galerie Beaujolais and peek over the lace half-curtains into the Louis XVI–Directoire interior of the restaurant that is now designated a national monument. It is lavish, expensive, and uniquely historic. The chef created special dishes named after Colette and Cocteau, who wrote:

There, at the bar, when the little cannon in the garden was fired and aroused a silky squall of pigeons like the ones in the Piazza San Marco, a few aborigines would assemble, happy to clink glasses together. . . . [Colette] could install herself at a table which bore her name, and add to the lustre of a place where some of the glories of France, from Fragonard to Balzac, had been guests.

Go back the few blocks to the avenue de l'Opera and the Métro Pyramides.

SCENE

T H E

FASHIONABLE

FAUBOURG

SIX

SCENE SIX

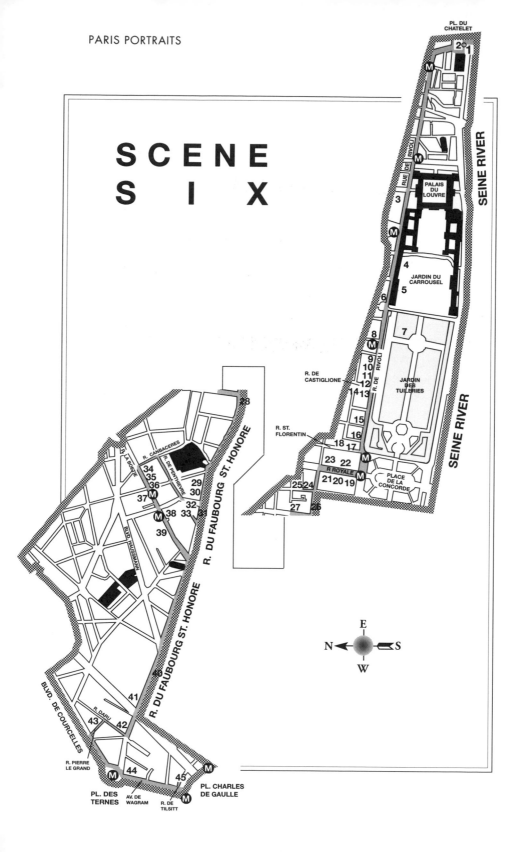

The River Seine marks the geographical and historical center of Paris. In the nineteenth century, besides lovers, anglers, painters, and bathers on the river banks, both sides of the Seine were covered with the barges, or *bateaux-lavoirs*, of the washerwomen of Paris. Here they lived and hung linen over the sides of the boats to beat it clean with a stick, and then dried it on lines strung across the large boats or on nearby fields. The literature of the nineteenth and twentieth centuries is rich in examples of the heroes in novels committing or contemplating suicide in the dirty yellowish-brown waters of the river. In Jean Rhys's *Quartet* (1928), as the heroine Mary Zelli stands on the quai des Orfèvres, near where this walk begins, a passing youth yells: "Hey, little one. Is it for tonight the suicide?"

If you arrive on the Métro, disembark at Châtelet, the largest station in Paris, then exit onto the place du Châtelet. For the first time on these strolls, you are next to the river. Remember, the streets that are sort of parallel to the Seine are numbered from east to west, following the current of the river; those that run perpendicular are numbered from the river outward, odd numbers on the left. The lovely square (now defined by two giant theaters) was formerly centered by the Grand Châtelet, the most vile of French prisons. The dreadful screams of the tortured prisoners and the blood-soaked cobblestones made this one of the most feared areas in Paris.

From here, walk on the rue de Rivoli past luxurious hotels to the fashionable and expensive rue du Faubourg-Saint-Honoré, site of many designer fashion houses. Save the Louvre Museum—which takes weeks, not hours, to view—for a later visit. First opened to the public in 1793 as an art gallery, this original palace of King Henry IV has been under construction, or reconstruction, since the sixteenth century. American writer Henry James described the interior in the latter part of the nineteenth century:

> *The pictures, the frames themselves, the figures within them, the particular parts and features of each, the look of the rich light, the smell of the massively enclosed, [all imparted] a sense of freedom of contact and appreciation.*

Amid loud controversy, a new modern entrance was inaugurated in 1988. American architect I. M. Pei's three glass pyramids cap a subterranean labyrinth of rooms leading to the classical old Louvre.

The proximity of the Louvre and the Tuileries, the lovely garden of the destroyed palace, was largely the reason many great hotels opened in this area. Fortunately, Paris laws protect the exterior of buildings, and no modern tower additions have been added to the elaborate hotels where some people lived permanently and English tourists and affluent Americans on the Grand Tour often stayed for months.

Métro Châtelet
Buses 38, 47, 58, 67, 69, 72

1. Théâtre du Châtelet
8, place du Châtelet

With a cast of mainly Italian singers, the New York Metropolitan Opera Company made its Paris début here on 21 May 1910 in a performance of *Aïda*. The great Toscanini conducted the orchestra, and Italian tenor Enrico Caruso starred in the successful opening night before a dazzling, bejeweled audience that included the French diplomatic corps and prosperous Americans such as the Vanderbilts and their friends. French jeweler Louis Cartier was present and valued jewelry worn by the elegantly dressed women at over three million dollars.

Sergei Diaghilev brought the Ballets Russes to Paris in 1909. (Photo by Lipnitzki, Bibliothèque Nationale.)

When Sergei Pavlovich Diaghilev introduced the magnificent dancers of the Imperial Russian Ballet to Paris on 19 May 1909, dancing had descended to a trivial appendage at the Paris opera house. In his determination to conquer Paris, he redecorated the Théâtre du Châtelet for his Ballets Russes. The sets by the painter Bakst, choreography by Fokine, the beauty and grace of the young Russian ballerinas, and the masculine strength of the male dancers, such as Vaslav Nijinsky, pounding out the rhythms of the Polovetsian Dances from Borodin's *Prince Igor* left the Paris society audience spellbound.

2. Formerly Théâtre Sarah-Bernhardt
1, place du Châtelet

At the age of fifty-five, in 1899, Sarah Bernhardt signed a twenty-five-year-lease on the Théâtre des Nations and renamed it after herself. She was to appear in the barn of a theater in forty different roles over the next sixteen years.

A complete renovation installed elegant yellow velvet hangings and yellow brocade padded walls in contrast to the ivory woodwork. The star's dressing room had cupboards large enough to hold fifty costumes at one time, a makeup table so extensive as to have an eight-paneled mirror, and an ornamental washbasin. The adjoining bathroom contained a huge tub that was usually overflowing with the flowers her admirers showered on her. At the bottom of a winding staircase, in the elegantly furnished dining room with a table that could seat twelve, Bernhardt greeted the crowds of admirers who burst backstage after each performance. A couple of times a week and on Sundays, she invited friends for a meal prepared in an adjoining complete kitchen. When Mme Bernhardt's ailing leg kept her from using the staircase, she frequently entertained on the stage amid the scenery.

When "the divine Sarah" died on 25 March 1921, her funeral cortège stopped on its slow journey from the church to Père-Lachaise cemetery for a minute of silent tribute outside her theater.

Cross to the west corner of the square, turn left onto the rue de Rivoli, and walk quite a distance.

3. Short-term residence of Mark Twain
164, rue de Rivoli

Turn the corner onto the place du Palais Royal and over what was the main entrance, carved in stone, is the name of the former luxury hotel that had once covered a whole block.

For three days in July 1867, Mark Twain stayed here in what he described as a "grand room" with a "sumptuous bed." He was beginning a trip to the Holy Land, which he later described in *Innocents Abroad* (1869):

> *Nearly one year has flown since this notable pilgrimage was ended; and as I sit here at home in San Francisco thinking, I am moved to confess that day by day the mass of memories of the excursion have grown more and more pleasant as the disagreeable incidents of travel which encumbered them flitted one by one out of my mind. . . . Travel is fatal to prejudice, bigotry, and narrow-mindedness, and many of our people need it sorely on these accounts. Broad, wholesome, charitable views of men and things cannot be acquired by vegetating in one little corner of the earth all one's lifetime.*

4. Musée des Arts Décoratifs
107, rue de Rivoli

Amid the many chairs, crystal, and porcelain that date from the period of Louis XVI through the nineteenth century are entire rooms of furnishings transferred intact from their original settings. Three rooms from the lavish apartment of Mme Jeanne Lanvin, founder of the couture House of Lanvin, are recreated with the original wallcoverings and furnishings. Madame's favorite theme—women— is illustrated in paintings by Degas, Renoir, Vuillard, and Boudin. The bedroom walls are covered in Shantung silk dyed "Lanvin blue," and the bath's hanging wall lamps are art-déco designs with sculptured marguerite flowers.

5. Musée National des Arts de la Mode
109, rue de Rivoli

Ten thousand costumes are in the museum devoted to fashion from the sixteenth to the twentieth centuries, including Brigitte Bardot's wedding dress and a gown made for Sarah Bernhardt. Some of the designer originals were donated by chic American socialites who, early on, patronized the French fashion industry. Besides the permanent collection displayed on the five floors, a major annual exhibition highlights the work of an important designer.

6. Short-term residence of A. J. Liebling
192, rue de Rivoli, Hôtel Regina

At the age of seven, the future writer and war correspondent A. J. Liebling stayed at this hotel with his younger sister and their German nanny. The summer heat was so severe that when walking they stayed on the sidewalk under the colonnade, and Liebling later wrote that for years afterward he thought of Paris as a city generally covered by a roof.

7. Jardin des Tuileries

Designed for Louis XIV in 1649, in 1906 the gardens were the starting point of what was to become the world's most prestigious balloon race. James Gordon Bennett, Jr., founder of the Paris *Herald*, sponsored the race that drew 250,000 spectators to watch sixteen gaily colored balloons representing six countries vie for the honor of flying the farthest distance before landing. Nowadays the three-day race is sponsored by the *International Herald Tribune*, successor of the original Paris paper, and is held at Vessy just outside Geneva, Switzerland.

8. Honeymoon site of Oscar Wilde
208, rue de Rivoli, Hôtel Wagram

Oscar Wilde and his bride Constance honeymooned here in the summer of 1884. Wrote Mrs. Wilde to her brother:

We have an appartement here of three rooms, 20 francs a day: not dear for a Paris hotel: we are au quatrième [on the fourth] and have a lovely view over the gardens of the Tuileries. . . .

9. Short-term residence of Mark Twain
218, rue de Rivoli, Hôtel Brighton

On another of his visits to Paris Mark Twain stayed here. He wanted to meet a *grisette* (a young woman of easy virtue) and, after he was shown dozens, wrote,

They were like nearly all the Frenchwomen I ever saw—homely. They had large hands, large feet, large mouths; they had pug-noses as a general thing, and mustaches that not even good breeding could overlook; they combed their hair straight back without parting; they were ill-shaped, they were not winning, they were not graceful; I knew by their looks that they ate garlic and onions; and lastly and finally, to my thinking it would be base flattery to call them immoral.

10. Couture shop of Madeleine Vionnet
222, rue de Rivoli

Considered by many to be the most innovative, intellectual, and, perhaps, the greatest couturière of all time, Mme Vionnet was the first to mold the dress to the natural body of the woman, not stuff the woman into the dress. Her modern bias-cut designs could be slipped over the head and worn without fasteners or undergarments.

From 1912 until she closed her business here during World War I, Vionnet, referred to as the Euclid of fashion, attracted sophisticated and cosmopolitan socialites such as the Queen of Belgium, Mrs. William K. Vanderbilt, and Elsie de Wolfe.

11. Formerly Rumpelmayer's
226, rue de Rivoli

This landmark pâtisserie, founded in 1908, is the place to stop for hot chocolate and cake. It was a favorite destination of Gertrude Stein and Alice B. Toklas on their afternoon walks from their Left Bank apartment. In 1946, Stein and her good friend Natalie Clifford Barney, after eating a disappointing lunch in a nearby restaurant, were caught entering Rumpelmayer's by a photographer, but Gertrude's rush for her favorite cake only allowed the cameraman to shoot a picture of her through the front window.

12. Dining site of Ernest and Pauline Hemingway
228, rue de Rivoli, Hôtel Meurice

When Hadley, the first Mrs. Ernest Hemingway, moved into her separate apartment with their young son in 1926, she signed an agreement giving Hemingway a divorce if, at the end of a hundred days of separation from Pauline Pfeiffer (assistant to the editor of Paris *Vogue* magazine), they still wished to marry. Having decided it would be easier for them to stay apart if an ocean was between them, Pauline and Hemingway spent their final night together at the elegant Meurice, where they dined on sole and partridge, before she sailed for New York on 24 September. After two months, Hadley called off the agreement with a letter to Ernest saying: "I took you originally for better, for worse (and meant it!) but in the case of your marrying some one else, I can stand by my vow only as an outside friend. . . . The three months separation is officially off." Hadley was given the royalties from *The Sun Also Rises* (1926), probably Hemingway's most successful novel.

Turn right at the corner.

13. Residences of M. F. K. Fisher and Janet Flanner
3, rue de Castiglione, formerly Hôtel Continental

In 1928, M. F. K. Fisher, famed for her writings about food, lived with her second husband in a vineyard set in a small village south of Geneva, Switzerland. To escape the freezing mountain winters, and because they missed the bustling city, the couple rented two small rooms in the attic servants' quarters in the old Continental. One of the closet-sized rooms was used as a workroom and storage for their books. While on a summer assignment for *Time-Life* magazines, Fisher returned to Paris twenty years later to find she could only rent one of the attic rooms in the now stylish and expensive hotel because Janet Flanner, the elderly columnist for *The New Yorker*, occupied their former bedroom. In Fisher's foreword to *The Alice B. Toklas Cookbook* (1954) she describes Flanner:

> *She was there, with her plain typing table, one beautiful cabinet of inlaid boiserie, always with a big fading garden bunch of roses or field flowers brought each weekend from her lover's country house, her little bathroom always hung with a drying elegant nightgown or some tiny high-style panties. There were perhaps a hundred books and no pictures, and her narrow bed made the little room seem almost austere, except for the hum of all Paris as it rose from far below, and the magnificent light that poured in and up from the Tuileries and the Seine and the Left Bank.*

"Letter from Paris," written under Flanner's pen name "Genêt," had appeared in *The New Yorker* since 1925. The columns were descriptive comments, written in a highly personal and colorful style, on what the French thought about events and people. Not long after the summer of 1958, an American airline purchased the hotel and remodeled it, forcing Flanner to move from the room where she said she truly felt at home.

14. Employment site of George Orwell
7, rue de Castiglione, Hôtel Lotti

What was it really like in the bowels and workrooms of a smart luxury hotel? George Orwell exposed his experiences in *Down and Out in Paris and London* (1933) after he worked in the kitchen here in 1919:

> *It was amusing to look round the filthy little scullery and think that only a double door was between us and the dining-room. There sat the customers in all their splendour—spotless table-cloths, bowls of flowers, mirrors and gilt cornices and painted cherubim; and here, just a few feet away, we in our disgusting filth.*

Retrace your steps back to rue de Rivoli.

15. Residence of Misia and Alfred Edwards
244, rue de Rivoli

As the mistress of Alfred Edwards, but still married to her first husband, Thadée Natanson, the extravagantly wealthy newspaper tycoon, Misia Natanson lived, in 1904, in a fashionable apartment behind the imposing carved wooden doors with brass lion's-head handles. The Louis XVI-style rooms, furnished with Louis XIV chairs and vast seventeenth-century tapestries, were lit by Venetian chandeliers. Footmen greeted Misia's guests, and butlers waited on them at her large dinner parties. It was a grand life of fashionable idleness. In 1905, both parties divorced their spouses and Misia officially became Mme Edwards.

16. Residence of José-María Sert
252, rue de Rivoli

After Misia and her second husband, Alfred Edwards, were divorced, she married the Spanish artist José-María Sert. Later, after their official parting, he remarried and was widowed. Misia and Sert stood on his balcony here to watch the Nazi troops goose-stepping in the place de la Concorde during the occupation of Paris in World War II. Sert died in 1945 and left the luxurious apartment and its furnishings to Misia. The antique furniture, a valuable library, and paintings and objets d'art kept Misia comfortably well off for the rest of her life; when she needed money, she sold the Louis XVI chairs or one of the grand commodes.

By the age of seventy-three, Misia was in very poor health and almost blind. She died here on 15 October 1950 immediately after seeing her closest friends: Chanel, Cocteau, and the distinguished writer-diplomat Paul Claudel.

17. Residence of Misia and Thadée Natanson
Rue Saint-Florentin, just off place de la Concorde

Just a few steps around the corner from the place of her death, the twenty-one-year-old Marie Sophie Olga Zenaide (Misia) Gkodebsky began married life in 1893 with her first husband, Thadée Natanson. As the wife of the young editor of *La revue blanche*, she knew everyone in the artistic and intellectual circles of Paris. Edouard Vuillard, in love with Misia, painted the fashionable young couple in the stylish flat decorated by Misia in supreme good taste. The *Salon with the Three Lamps* (1894) pictures M. Natanson sitting in a bentwood rocker placed in a room with patterned wallpaper, a paisley Spanish shawl draped across Misia's piano, the floors covered in gaily patterned oriental carpets. The Natansons collected paintings by their friends, none of whom were notable at the time; in 1908, Thadée, in financial straits, sold nineteen Bonnards and twenty-seven Vuillards, as well as works by Cézanne, Delacroix, Daumier, Seurat, and Vallotton.

Place de la Concorde about 1910. (From Paris Illustrated, *courtesy of Thomas Gee.)*

18. Couture shop of Jean Patou
7, rue Saint-Florentin

Patou originated many of the haute couture symbols now associated with French designers. He was the first to make a social event of the fashion show by inviting favorite friends and the press and serving them a champagne supper. Decorating his clothes, purses, and scarves with his personal initials—now commonly the hallmark of most designers—was as innovative in the twenties as was opening a store named Coin des Sports (Corner of Sports) at this location completely devoted to outfits and accessories for outdoor activity.

The society hostess Elsa Maxwell worked with Patou to perfect his perfume Joy (still one of the most expensive scents), and said he had more animal magnetism than anyone she ever met. Today the House of Patou is still run by members of his family.

You'll want to stop in the busy place de la Concorde and, like the hero in Henry James's *The Tragic Muse* (1890), look over "the great square, the opposite bank of the Seine, the steep blue roofs of the quay, the bright immensity of Paris."

Double back to enter place de la Concorde.

19. Hôtel Crillon
10, place de la Concorde

Many illustrious Americans have stayed at the luxurious Crillon, including Mary Pickford and Douglas Fairbanks on their honeymoon in 1920 and Private James Thurber in 1918. The dancer Isadora Duncan and the only lover she married, Russian poet Serge Esenin, stayed here in 1920 upon returning from an American tour that scandalized proper Boston Brahmins when Isadora bared her breasts to the audience. The management of the Crillon asked Isadora to move after they had to call the police on Esenin, who smashed up the room during a bout of heavy drinking.

Retrace your steps back to rue Royale.

20. Maxim's
3, rue Royale

"I'm going to Maxim's," sang the male star of Franz Lehar's prototype Belle Epoque operetta *The Merry Widow* (1905). Only the most successful artists and writers, such as F. Scott Fitzgerald and Sinclair Lewis, and the wealthy patrons of the arts dined in the lavish rococo restaurant. In *Being Geniuses Together* (1968), Robert McAlmon writes of the time English author Ronald Firbank, after imbibing a dozen cocktails, asked that a taxi be called to take him to Maxim's. Firbank had eaten nothing since the day before and since he never ate, but only drank, McAlmon didn't know why he wanted to go to Maxim's.

21. Couture shop of Edward Molyneux
5, rue Royale

In the twenties and thirties, the Irish Molyneux designed for fashionable women who wanted to be dressed perfectly correctly. In just two years he became such a success that, in 1921, he moved his salon here to larger quarters in rooms decorated in shades of gray with crystal chandeliers and furnished with Louis XVI chairs.

Furs, lingerie, hats, gowns, and perfumes were designed by Molyneux in the years before World War II. Just before Paris fell to the Germans in 1940, he escaped to England on a coal barge, returning in a more conventional manner in 1945.

Life in Paris was not the same; his health was fading, his greatest competitors, Chanel and Vionnet, were retired, and Patou was dead. When the House of Molyneux closed in 1952, Molyneux returned to his love of art—collecting and painting subtly colored landscapes. He is mostly remembered as the designer who helped shape the thirties look of higher waists and lower hemlines.

22. Design house of Louiseboulanger
6, rue Royale

Marlene Dietrich was described as "leaning against a wall in a Louiseboulanger green velvet tunic richly bordered in sable." Around the close of 1934, Louiseboulanger (first and last names run together) moved her design house to these modern rooms that were a more appropriate background for her innovative designs. In 1939, she closed her fashion house, remarking: "The day tennis came in, the demimondaine went out, and fashion went with her."

23. Couture shop of Molyneux
14, rue Royale

When Edward Molyneux first moved to Paris from England in 1919, he opened his haute couture house with the help of wealthy British backers. From the beginning he was known for his perfect taste and simplicity of designs, and it wasn't long before he expanded to larger quarters across the street.

Turn left at the corner.

24. Design house of Jeanne Lanvin
22, rue du Faubourg-Saint-Honoré

The House of Lanvin is still located where, in a two-room apartment, the twenty-three-year-old milliner originally set up shop in 1890. For fifty years, Mme Lanvin produced haute couture emphasizing femininity and elegance. Even during the flapper years, when women wished to de-emphasize the curves of the body, Lanvin stated that "modern clothes need some sort of romantic quality," and she continued to produce fanciful dreamy dresses throughout the twenties and thirties.

Since Lanvin's death in 1946, the House of Lanvin has continued to be directed by a member of her family. Perhaps Lanvin's greatest contributions to French fashion were the designs that showed women could be eternally youthful; they no longer had to dress according to their age or stage in life but could be a certain "type"—girlish, athletic, exotic, "smart"—and carry this look throughout life.

Turn right around the corner.

Fashion designer Jeanne Lanvin around 1930.
(Photo by Laure Albin-Goyot, courtesy of Lanvin, Inc.)

25. Le Boeuf sur le Toit
28, rue Boissy-d'Anglas

The "Ox on the Roof" cabaret opened with a spectacular party on 10 January 1922 at which Cocteau, Brancusi, Pablo and Olga Picasso, and Marie Laurencin danced on the small crowded dance floor to the jazz piano of Jean Wiener. This was the second location for the dada-inspired club named for the circus-ballet concocted by Cocteau and Darius Milhaud with colorful sets by Raoul Dufy.

The patrons of the club drew dada sketches on the bare walls. Everyone —*tout Paris* — patronized Le Boeuf, either to eat the twenty-four-franc meal, to drink in the eclectic ambiance, or to be seen with the likes of King Ferdinand of Rumania.

When art collector Peggy Guggenheim and writer Laurence Vail (king of Paris's bohemia) were married in 1920 at the town hall of the sixteenth arrondissement, Guggenheim's internationally known mother hosted a party at the Hôtel Plaza-Athénée. Later that evening the more bohemian friends of the bride and groom were entertained at a second wedding celebration at Le Boeuf. Among the guests were Helen Fleischman, later to marry James Joyce's son George, and Guggenheim's cousin Harold Loeb, later satirized as Robert Cohn in Hemingway's *The Sun Also Rises* (1926).

26. Residence of Coco Chanel
29, rue du Faubourg-Saint-Honoré

Press the large button and enter through the tall wooden doors to the interior garden of the building with a glass canopy covering the entrance.

By 1925, the House of Chanel was so successful that Mademoiselle could afford to live in a sumptuous ground-floor apartment in this aristocratic hôtel particulier. Her good friend Picasso was welcomed at any hour to stay in the room saved specially for him. Chanel and Picasso first met at one of Misia Sert's fashionable parties and the designer was "swept up by a passion for him. . . . He had a way of looking at me. . . . I trembled."

When Cocteau produced his adaptation of *Antigone* (1923) he chose Picasso to do the sets, Paul Honegger to compose the music, and Chanel to design the costumes because "she is our leading dressmaker and I cannot imagine Oedipus' daughters patronizing a 'little dressmaker.'" The newspaper reviewers, proclaiming that Chanel had gone Greek, raved over the costumes and sets.

Take a right turn.

Coco Chanel around 1925. By this time, the House of Chanel was extremely successful. (Photo by Horst, courtesy of Chanel, Paris.)

27. Residence of Jean Cocteau
10, rue d'Anjou

Jean and his devoted mother shared a stately apartment close to his beloved friend and patron, Chanel. The affluent Mme Cocteau kept a refined household with a butler guarding the interior doors. You can step inside the entrance foyer and see the well-preserved nineteenth-century original heating stoves and the fine wood panelling and broad staircase. For entertaining his sometimes raucous friends, Cocteau kept a room at a nearby small hotel. Gertrude Stein said he prided himself on being eternally thirty.

28. Birthplace of W. Somerset Maugham
39, rue du Faubourg-Saint-Honoré, British Embassy

On 25 January 1874, the British Embassy was the setting for the birth of Maugham, son of a prosperous English lawyer. French law stated that anyone born on French soil was automatically a French citizen and could be conscripted into the French armed services, so the British turned one wing of the embassy into a maternity ward for British nationals. In Maugham's *The Razor's Edge* (1944), the narrator shows a woman friend the seamier side of Paris: "It is a dingy narrow street and even as you enter it you get the impression of sordid lust."

29. Couture house of Marcel Rochas
100, rue du Faubourg-Saint-Honoré

M. Rochas opened his couture house on the place Beauvau in 1925, supposedly to provide his beautiful young wife with attractive clothing. The Rochas motto—youth, simplicity, and individuality—was so successful that six years later he moved the house into larger quarters. The first pantsuit for women was conceived by Rochas in 1932, with a grey flannel jacket-and-pants outfit to be worn on city streets. He claimed to have invented the word "slacks." Actresses Joan Crawford and Mae West wore Rochas designs.

30. Short-term residence of Sinclair Lewis
112, rue du Faubourg-Saint-Honoré, Bristol Hôtel

The year *Arrowsmith* (1925) was published, Sinclair Lewis wrote parts of *Elmer Gantry* (1927), his satirical novel about religious bigotry in the United States, while staying at the Bristol. When the Nobel Prize was awarded to Lewis in 1930, writer Robert McAlmon noted:

> *I recall not a paragraph written by Lewis which gives me a joy in its velocity or suggestive quality. He is too intent on types to depict character. However, the world has become accustomed to seeing the Nobel Prize given to writers of second and third rank. It is pleasing to the populace, the mediocre.*

31. Couture house of Grès
83, rue du Faubourg-Saint-Honoré

After changing her hated first name to Alix, Germaine Barton opened the couture house of Alix in 1934. Although she left the firm six years later, the name stayed because she didn't own the copyright. Now she used the professional name of her painter husband, Grès, and the House of Grès was established at a new location. Alix Barton (Grès) was to became famous for her timeless draped jersey creations, most of which would be stylish today.

32. Couture house of Pierre Cardin
118, rue du Faubourg-Saint-Honoré

Cardin worked for Schiaparelli, Paquin, and Christian Dior before opening his own business in 1950. In 1954, Eve, a boutique just for women, expanded at this location. In the seventies, *Time* magazine wrote that Cardin was "that shrewd fanaticist who has tacked his name onto just about anything that can be nailed, glued, backed, molded, bolted, braced, bottled, opened, shut, pushed, and pulled." The article referred to his 506 licenses in 93 countries, including a chain of restaurants worldwide.

Cardin is an inventive couturier, paying special attention to construction. His early designs precursed the sack dress, and by the sixties he was showing vinyl dresses appropriate for wearing on a spaceship destined for Mars.

33. Couture house of Charles Frederick Worth and Paquin
120, rue du Faubourg-Saint-Honoré

The fourth generation of Worths showed their first collection at this address in 1936. They inherited much from founder Charles Frederick Worth, including the merging of impeccable English tailoring with French chic, thus setting the standard of elegance in women's fashion for almost a hundred years. Like most couture houses, they were forced to close during World War II. At the end of the war, the Paris House of Worth merged with Paquin.

Mme Paquin had retired in the thirties, and the business then produced almost nothing but fur-trimmed coats. It was clear that its talented founder and designer was missed. The combined Worth and Paquin closed permanently in 1956. All that remains today of the House of Worth is the name on toiletries for men and women.

34. Residence of Henry James
19, rue La Boétie

In his 1913 story, "A Small Boy and Others," Henry James described the scene below the windows of the apartment his family lived in from September 1856 to the following spring. The bakery where they bought the morning's "soft and crusty crescent-rolls" was at the corner, and the blue-and-white crémerie was next door to the oyster-lady, who with "her paraphernalia, fitted into their interstice much as the mollusc itself into its shell."

35. Formerly Paul Rosenberg Gallery
21, rue La Boétie

After a summer in Saint-Raphael on the Mediterranean, Picasso returned to Paris in 1919 with his recent bride, the Russian ballerina Olga Koklova. Paul Rosenberg was then his agent, and on 20 October Picasso's drawings of open windows, through which shone the bright côte d'Azur sun, were placed on exhibition. The invitation featured Picasso's first lithograph, and a drawing of Olga in front of a closed window appeared on the cover of the catalogue. The large group at the showing loved Picasso's neoclassical realistic work as a break from cubist still-lifes. As Picasso said of himself: "Whenever I had something to say I have said it in the manner in which I have felt it ought to be said."

36. Residence of Pablo and Olga Picasso
23, rue La Boétie

This busy street was lined with antique shops and modern art dealers when the Picassos moved into a large apartment in this building. Success brought them upper-middle-class respectability. Gone was the bohemian clutter and freedom Picasso had relished in Montmartre. Instead of wearing the paint-stained corduroy trousers of a bohemian artist, Picasso now dressed in a dinner jacket with a bullfighter's cummerbund and a gold watch in his vest pocket to the countless fashionable dinners attended by Olga's society friends. Olga's insistence on fastidiousness drove Picasso to rent another apartment for his studio and storeroom—one flight up the steep stairs, under the eaves of the roof. In the room he used as a studio, "the window faced south and offered a beautiful view of the rooftops of Paris, bristling with a forest of red and black chimneys, with the slender, far-off silhouette of the Eiffel Tower rising between them" (Braissai, *Picasso and Company 1966*). The outside door to this studio was always locked; no one, especially Olga, was allowed in unless specifically invited.

When Americans Gerald and Sara Murphy were invited to view his paintings in various stages of completion, crammed into every room, Picasso led Gerald to an alcove in which sat a tall cardboard box full of illustrations, photographs, engravings, and articles clipped from newspapers. All were about a single subject—Abraham Lincoln. He had been collecting them since he was a child.

Holding up one of Brady's photographs of Lincoln, Picasso said with great emotion: "There is the real American elegance!"

Pablo Picasso, Portrait of Olga in an Armchair, *1917.*
(La Réunion des Musées Nationaux by SPADEM.)

37. Couture house of Jacques Fath
32, rue La Boétie

Fath's first couture collection in 1937 consisted of twenty pieces of clothing displayed in two rooms so crowded that customers and models spilled out into the courtyard. In just two years he became one of Paris's most promising new designers and moved to larger quarters here.

For almost fifteen years, Fath designed elegant evening gowns that moved with the wearer, clean-cut designs for daytime wear, and novel accessories. Perhaps his best-known client was the late American film star Rita Hayworth, for whom he made a wedding dress and trousseau when she married Prince Aly Khan.

38. Meeting place of Gustav Mahler and Auguste Rodin
45, rue la Boétie, Salle Gaveau

Gustav Mahler's First Symphony was premièred at this auditorium in 1909 and the Austrian composer was first introduced here to the music-loving French sculptor Auguste Rodin. Very often Rodin found inspiration for his work in music and is quoted as saying: "If by methods of his art a sculptor succeeded in suggesting impressions that literature or music ordinarily provide, why pick a quarrel with him?"

39. Residence of John Singer Sargent
52, rue La Boétie

Music was also important to the work of Sargent, an exceedingly proficient pianist. When subjects sitting for portraits appeared uneasy, Sargent relaxed them by playing as a break from painting. Sargent was born in Italy to American parents, and the family lived here in 1874. At the age of eighteen, he had already studied painting in Italy for two years but had yet to visit the country of his citizenship.

Turn right at the corner with the church.

40. Residence of Honoré de Balzac
191, rue du Faubourg-Saint-Honoré

Like Charles Dickens, Balzac was a genius whose works have been translated into more languages than those of any other writer of the early nineteenth century. His most famous novel, *La comédie humaine* (1842–48), recreates French society of the time, picturing in great detail characters representative of every class and profession. He died in this house in 1850.

41. Residence of Gustave Flaubert
240, rue du Faubourg-Saint-Honoré

After an aging Flaubert moved here in the 1870s, his friends attended Sunday afternoon salons in the white-and-gold fourth-floor drawing room. The group of brilliant writers, including Zola, Turgenev, Edmond and Jules de Goncourt, and Daudet, conversed on various subjects as their host stood in front of the mantelpiece, which held a large gilded statue of the Buddha. As the novelist excitedly spoke, he burst "with tremendous paradoxes" and "shook his two fists at the ceiling."

42. Performance hall for George Antheil
252, rue du Faubourg-Saint-Honoré, Salle Pleyel

This performance hall was rented in 1925 by George Antheil for a semiprivate preview of his *Ballet méchanique*. After arranging for publicity, renting at least three player pianos, and acquiring Bravig Imbs to play in his place, Antheil disappeared to Africa, supposedly in search of "new rhythms." He was really hiding out in Tunis, creating wide publicity with his presumed disappearance.

Just as arranged, the preview went on without him but with his friends Sylvia Beach, Adrienne Monnier, James Joyce, and Elliot Paul in attendance. As the pianos played the wild loud chords, Imbs, dressed in a black-and-orange jacket, performed in Antheil's place. He later wrote that there was a "gasp of relief" when a music roll finished.

Turn right at the corner.

43. Marriage site of Pablo and Olga Picasso
Rue Daru, Eglise Saint-Alexandre-Nevsky

Gertrude Stein, Alice B. Toklas, Matisse, Braque, Diaghilev, Léonide Massine, and Paul Rosenberg were among the celebrants here on 12 July 1917, at the marriage of Picasso and Olga Koklova. The splendid Russian Orthodox ceremony was replete with much pomp and circumstance, flowers, incense, and candles. The Picassos had wed earlier in a civil ceremony at the town hall of the seventh arrondissement on the Left Bank with Max Jacob, Cocteau, and Apollinaire as witnesses.

In remembrance of the marriage, Picasso gave Gertrude Stein a "lovely little" painting which, many years later, Toklas copied in needlework for a small footstool.

From his honeymoon in Biarritz, Picasso wrote to Apollinaire: "I've decorated a room with your poems. I'm not too unhappy here and I work as I have told you, but write to me long letters." In May, Picasso had served as a witness when Apollinaire married Jacqueline Kolb. By 9 November his longtime dear friend Apollinaire would be dead of Spanish influenza.

44. Residence of Augustus Saint-Gaudens
233, rue du Faubourg-Saint-Honoré, 3 bis, villa Wagram Saint-Honoré

Turn in through the gates and walk up the hill.

This is one of those charming, quiet, tiny lanes hidden all over Paris. The American sculptor Augustus Saint-Gaudens, best known for his public monuments, lived here in a first-floor studio in 1877, but by 1906 he had moved to the Left Bank, where there were larger inexpensive work spaces for sculptors. He died the next year.

45. Residence of F. Scott and Zelda Fitzgerald
14, rue de Tilsitt

When Scott and Zelda Fitzgerald moved to a fifth-floor apartment here on 22 April 1925, he was at the height of his fame, having already accomplished his best work. He later described the summer of 1925 as "one of 1,000 parties and no work." They had returned from a year's stay in Saint-Raphael on the Mediterranean and, even though his books and short stories were selling well, he had, as usual, spent more than his $116,000 previous year's royalties.

Zelda described the furnishings of the somber apartment as "early Galleries Lafayette" (still the major Paris department store) and reported it to be none too clean. Faded gold-and-purple wallpaper and damp rooms with an air of neglect contributed to a feeling of lost elegance.

This is practically the beginning of the next walk, but if you wish to save it for another time, you can catch the Métro at the Charles de Gaulle Etoile stop at the Arc de Triomphe, just ahead.

F. Scott and Zelda Fitzgerald with their daughter, Scotty, in their Paris apartment, Christmas 1925. (Princeton University Library.)

SCENE

IMAGES
OF
ELEGANCE

SEVEN

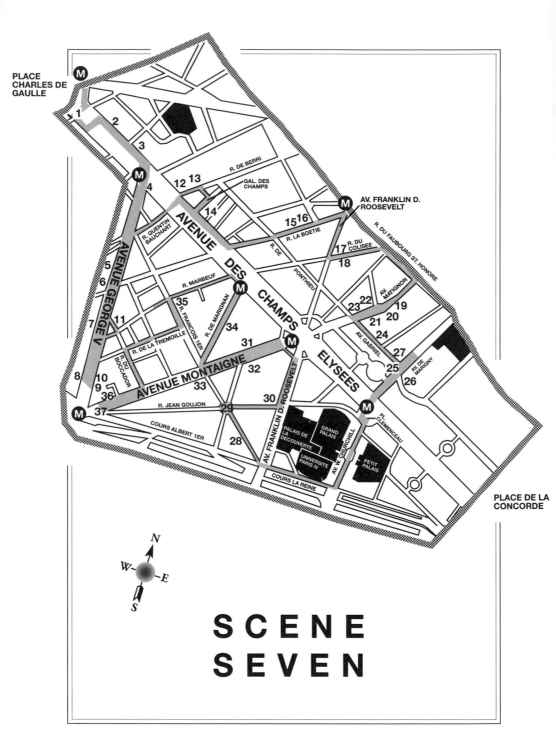

SCENE
SEVEN

Along with Park Avenue in New York City, the Champs-Elysées in Paris is probably the most renowned avenue in the western world. South from the rond-point to the terminus at the place de la Concorde, the broad thoroughfare is bordered by immaculate sweeping lawns dotted with old chestnut trees, luxuriant azalea bushes, and occasional exclusive restaurants in Louis XVI buildings with summer terraces. A young Marcel Proust was sent by his mother to play in the gardens; he later wrote of his feelings: "Going there I found unendurable."

By the latter half of the nineteenth century, large elegant mansions and fashionable cafés still lined the avenue; it was where the beau monde went to be seen. Use your imagination while walking on the crowded sidewalks and search for the buildings behind the added façades. You will find nineteenth-century beauty behind the garish neon marquées of airline offices, automobile showrooms, fast-food emporiums, and movie palaces.

The original hôtel particulier at number 25, once the home of a Polish adventuress, is famous for its genuine onyx staircase. Numbers 71–79 were the Hôtel Choiseu-Gouffier, demolished to build the rue Lincoln, but in 1856 home to financier Emile Girardin at the time he entertained Charles Dickens. In a letter to a friend, Dickens wrote about the

> *three gorgeous drawing rooms with ten thousand wax candles in golden sconces, terminating in a dining room of unprecedented magnificence with two enormous transparent plate-glass doors in it, looking (across an antechamber full of clean plates) straight into the kitchen, with the cooks in their white paper caps dishing the dinner.*

Enduring, serene, aristocratic streets lined with high-fashion houses, selective galleries, and deluxe hotels radiate from the avenue as it flows to the Arc de Triomphe, built by the Emperor Napoléon to honor his army. Today the arch is an honored memorial to France's war dead. Under the memorial flame which is lit each evening at 6:30 P.M. lies the unknown soldier of World War I. Each 14 July a military parade commemorates the fall of the hated Bastille prison and the founding of the First French Republic. On 26 August 1944, General Charles de Gaulle led thousands of armed forces and military bands down the Champs in celebration of the liberation of Paris from the Nazis, as hundreds of thousands of French onlookers cried and cheered.

For the celebration of the 200th anniversary of the storming of the Bastille, on the evening of 14 July 1989, a $15-million, three-hour extravaganza promenaded past two million onlookers massed on the Champs-Elysées between the Etoile and the place de la Concorde. Besides elephants, horses painted to look like zebras, a ninety-foot steam-belching train engine with twenty men pounding on oil drums, eight thousand extras, and three thousand French soldiers, the show included the Florida A&M Marching Band representing the United States.

More than French military demonstrations have gathered around the arch. American poet e. e. cummings attended a political array one afternoon in 1924:

> *16 eures*
> *l'etoile*
> *the communists have fine eyes*
> *some are young some old none*
> *look alike the flics rush*
> *batter the crowd sprawls collapses . . .*

My inauguration to the Champs-Elysées was at night, when the myriads of brightly colored lights that proclaim Paris to be the City of Lights masked the tackiness. As I crossed the pont de la Concorde from the Left Bank, I could see the Arc de Triomphe in the distance, the Tour Eiffel looming to its left; and when I turned into the avenue from the place de la Concorde, where King Louis XVI lost his head under the guillotine, I was stunned by the beauty of the expanse of Paris before my eyes. Practically jogging, I kept repeating to my companion, "We are walking on the Champs-Elysées!"

> *Today it is lovely again and along the Champs-Elysées at twilight it is like an outdoor seraglio choked with dark-eyed houris [beauties]. The trees are in full foliage and of a verdure so pure, so rich, that it seems as though they were still wet and glistening with dew. From the Palais du Louvre to the Etoile it is like a piece of music for the pianoforte. (Henry Miller)*

Métro Etoile Charles de Gaulle
Buses 92, 73, 31, 30

Of course you will want to visit the monumental arch in the place Charles-de-Gaulle. Then walk under the busy intersection via the pedestrian passage to the west side of the Champs-Elysées.

1. Former residence of Grace Moore (133), avenue des Champs-Elysées, formerly Hôtel Astoria

The original building burned down in 1972, forty-three years after soprano Grace Moore resided there in an apartment when appearing in Puccini's opera *La bohème*. While Moore sang the role of Mimi in Italian, the rest of the cast sang in the original French.

2. Couture house of Maggy Rouff 136, avenue des Champs-Elysées

Maggy de Wagner continued her mother's trade as a designer of sportswear when she opened the couture house of Maggy Rouff in 1929. She worked as the sole designer until her retirement in 1948, when the house moved to a new location.

The Champs-Elysées about 1910. (*From* Paris Illustrated, *courtesy of Thomas Gee.*)

The Rouff designs were at once elegant, imaginative, and feminine; her crisply tailored sportswear of the late twenties was advertised as a "peep in the future." Known as an intelligent woman, Maggy published two books: *America Seen through a Microscope*, about her trip to the United States, and *The Philosophy of Elegance*, a subject she knew well: "Style is like love, it can happen in a flash or develop over a long period."

3. Office of James Gordon Bennett, Jr. 120, avenue des Champs-Elysées

The head editorial offices of the Paris *Herald* were in this mansion, where publisher James Gordon Bennett, Jr., received important visitors, *not* including Theodore Roosevelt and William Randolph Hearst. These names were on the infamous list of people whom he banned forever from the *Herald*.

Tall and lanky with a handlebar mustache, the independent publisher made journalistic history when he sent Henry Stanley to Africa to find Dr. Livingston.

4. Favorite café of James Joyce 99, avenue des Champs-Elysées, Le Fouquet

The glittering old café-restaurant was almost demolished in 1988 but was saved by designation as a historical monument. In 1936, James Joyce liked to dine here with his family and, since he was nearly blind, the waiter read the menu out loud to him. Joyce ate very lightly and simply—mushrooms, oysters, and lobsters—but always encouraged his family and friends to choose the finest food on the menu. Nora Joyce, his wife, enjoyed food more—especially fancy desserts.

Nancy Cunard, the English shipping heiress, when invited to join the Joyces at Fouquet's, could not find them behind their clutter of lobster shells and wine bottles. As she searched the noisy rooms, wondering why the Joyces patronized a place favored by horse-racing people and smart society, she worried that "Mrs. Joyce would be furious with her for being late."

One night Nora pointed out Marlene Dietrich to her husband, who then rose and visited Dietrich's nearby table, introducing himself by declaring his admiration for her in the movie *The Blue Angel*. Dietrich replied: "Then, monsieur, you saw me at my best."

Sylvia Beach reported that Joyce was an overgenerous tipper and hence was very popular in restaurants. "The waiters, and the boy who fetched him a taxi, all those who served him, must have retired with a fortune."

5. Couture house of Jean Dessès
37, avenue George-V

After the Egyptian-born Dessès opened his couture house here in 1937, he became famous for his intricately draped chiffon evening dresses. Noted clients included the royal women of Greece and the Duchess of Windsor.

6. Short-term residence of Duke Ellington
31, avenue George-V, Hôtel George V

Duke Ellington, playing at the Salle Pleyel in July 1933, stayed in an apartment so large and with so many doors leading to other rooms that it took him five minutes to find his way out. American jazz was so popular in Paris in the twenties and thirties that, at the intermission of one of his concerts, a group of Parisian society people invited to join Ellington backstage at a buffet reception caused such a crush that a duchess lost an extremely valuable ring. As the musicians and guests joined in the hunt, the duchess exclaimed: "I can always get diamonds, but how often can I get a Duke Ellington?"

7. Services for Bennett, Jr., and Gertrude Stein
23, avenue George-V, The American Cathedral

Two solemn rituals for Americans who lived in Paris were conducted at this Episcopal church built in 1887: the marriage of James Gordon Bennett, Jr., in 1914 and the funeral of Gertrude Stein in 1946.

Bennett was married on 10 September, at the age of seventy-three, to the former Maud Potter of Philadelphia, widow of George de Reuter of Reuters news service. When Bennett died four years later, *Editor and Publisher* magazine named him "the world's most famous newspaper-maker," but on an inside page changed it to "the most conspicuous newspaper-maker in the world."

Although Gertrude Stein died of stomach cancer on 27 July 1946 in the American Hospital, she was not buried until 22

October. Her body lay in a vault in the church until the ceremony of prayers was read by Dean Beekman; after which her immediate survivors, Alice B. Toklas and Allan Stein, son of her brother Michael, accompanied her body to cimetière Père-Lachaise for burial. English artist Francis Rose designed the massive rectangular headstone that now reads on one side "Gertrude Stein, San Francisco" and on the other side simply, "Alice B. Toklas." On All Saints Day, Stein admirers of various nationalities gather to remember the writer who said that America was her country but Paris was her home.

8. Couture house of Hubert James Taffin de Givenchy
3, avenue George-V

After many years of apprenticeship with the leading designers, Givenchy opened a maison de couture in 1953, moving it here in 1955, just across the street from his mentor, Balenciaga, who "taught me it isn't necessary to put a button where it doesn't belong, or to add a flower to make a dress beautiful. It is beautiful of itself."

Givenchy's cheerfully colored designs appear deceptively simple. With Balenciaga, he pioneered the sheath dress and the chemise. Givenchy's costumes worn by actress Audrey Hepburn in many of her American movies influenced generations of women.

9. Couture house of Cristóbal Balenciaga
10, avenue George-V

According to *Harper's Bazaar* in 1938, Balenciaga's was the couture house to patronize if a woman wanted a dress that "fitted the figure like a wet glove." Born in the Basque mountains of Spain, he might never have emigrated to Paris had it not been for the Spanish Civil War. For over thirty years his shop "was a monastery, architectural and spiritual" that represented innovation and perfection. The clothes, designed with severity but with an ease of fit, were worn by the world's most elegant women, including Mrs. Paul Mellon and Gloria Guinness.

The reclusive Balenciaga lived for and loved his work. Besides the sack dress, he introduced to the fashion world the kimono coat and the tunic. He was a designer's designer. "Balenciaga is the only real couturier," Chanel declared. "He alone is capable of cutting the fabric, mounting it, of sewing it with his own hands. The others are just designers." She was one of his few close friends until, following a quarrel, Balenciaga sent back all her gifts like a spurned lover.

An important chapter in French fashion ended in 1972 when Balenciaga died, four years after he closed the business.

10. Couture house of Mainboucher
12, avenue George-V

As the only American to successfully launch a haute couture house in Paris, Mainboucher attracted the American upper class seeking the ladylike look. His salons were exquisitely detailed: zebra-skin rugs, mirrors, porcelains, and fresh flowers. As the Second World War neared, he closed this location and returned to America. Undoubtedly his most famous client had been Wallis Simpson, whose wedding dress he designed for her marriage to the Duke of Windsor.

11. Residences of Art Buchwald and Theodore White
24, rue du Boccador

After World War II, two American writers occupied apartments in this handsome five-story building. The manager, a nephew of the two elderly women owners, ruled that occupants were allowed to ascend in the elevator but never to descend, making frequent spot checks when the owners heard "the sorrowful creaking of the cables in the elevator shaft," reported former occupant Irwin Shaw.

Buchwald occupied a studio on the top floor next to the room of his future wife Ann McGarry. In 1949 he wrote the "Paris after Dark" column for the New York *Herald Tribune*—not as an expatriate like the Americans of Montparnasse in the twenties, but as a United States citizen who happened to be in France. His occasional studies at the Alliance française were financed by the G.I. Bill for veterans of World War II.

Much of Theodore White's Pulitzer Prize-winning book, *The Mountain Road* (1958), was written between 1948 and 1953 when he lived in Paris as the European correspondent for *The Reporter*. White had resigned as chief of staff of the China bureau of *Time* magazine in order to complete his book about World War II, and in 1953, *Fire in Ashes: Europe in Mid-Century* was published.

12. Couture house of Louiseboulanger
3, rue de Berri

In 1923, Louise Boulanger ran her two names together and opened the maison de couture decorated in the modern style reflective of her innovative designs. At this time, a Paris guidebook stated: "Women who dare to wear clothes that are strikingly individual and about three seasons ahead of the style naturally gravitate toward Louiseboulanger." The business relocated on the rue Royale in 1934.

13. Short-term residence of Helen Keller
7, rue de Berri, Hôtel Lancaster

Miss Helen Keller, blind and deaf from the age of two, graduated from Radcliffe College in 1904. *The Story of My Life* (1902) chronicles her four-day stay here in 1937. She had originally come to Paris to attend the unveiling of a statue of Thomas Paine, but since this had already occurred, Gutzon Borglum, sculptor of the three presidents at Mount Rushmore, led her on an unforgettable tour of the Musée Rodin. Upon viewing *The Thinker* with her hands, she exclaimed: "In every limb I felt the throes of emerging mind."

14. Meeting place of Ernest Walsh and Ethel Moorhead
74, avenue des Champs-Elysées, formerly Hôtel Claridge

In 1925, the most influential literary journal of the American expatriate colony was *This Quarter*, edited by poet Ernest Walsh and backed by his much older wife, Ethel Moorhead. The couple met at the hotel's bar when the destitute Walsh's luggage was confiscated because he couldn't pay his bill. Over drinks (she paid), after revealing to her that he was ill with consumption, Walsh said, "I'm fine. I've got another five years to live." He died in Monte Carlo the next year at the age of thirty-one.

15. Exhibit by Joan Miró
110, rue La Boétie, Galerie Lécarne

Two years after the young Spanish artist Joan Miró followed fellow artist Picasso to Paris, Dr. Girarden, a dentist and owner of this gallery, sponsored a show of Miró's work during the first two weeks of May 1921. Although no paintings were sold, the artist was not discouraged. "Of art," he said, "I love it as the only end of my life."

16. Paul Guillaume's gallery
108, rue La Boétie

"It's a peach!" exclaimed American Albert Barnes in 1922, upon viewing a portrait by Chaim Soutine of a clownlike pastry chef. Gallery owner Guillaume understood little English and had never heard this idiomatic expression. He replied, "*Non*, it's a pastry chef!" Barnes purchased all of Soutine's exhibited works and demanded to meet the painter. The encounter was unpleasant, and years later the artist called the wealthy, cantankerous collector a boor. Barnes's purchases of the paintings made Soutine a celebrity. Works by Renoir, Picasso, Cézanne and Matisse also hang in the Barnes Foundation in Merion, Pennsylvania, outside Philadelphia.

17. Shop of Peggy Guggenheim and Mina Loy
Rue du Colisée

American heiress Peggy Guggenheim, a patron of twentieth-century modern art, sailed for Europe in 1920, married writer Lawrence Vail in Paris, and stayed on for twenty-one more years. At a shop somewhere on this street, she sold inventive lampshades designed by her friend Mina Loy. One shade was a globe of the world with a light inside it, another was a boat whose sails were down, and a third style was a double-cellophane shade with paper cutouts in between which "cast beautiful shadows."

18. Le Boeuf sur le Toit
34, rue du Colisée

The original twenties restaurant with the dada-inspired décor is now a chain of five situated in various Paris locations. A dying Marcel Proust declared: "If I could only be well enough to go once to the cinema, and to Le Boeuf sur le Toit."

19. Couture house of Lucien Lelong
16, avenue Matignon

When Nora Joyce patronized Lelong at his design house here, a typical outfit cost between 750 and 1,450 francs. This was a tremendous expense for the wife of James Joyce, whose works did not sell widely until *Ulysses* was purchased by Random House in 1932.

20. Couture house of Jacques Heim
15, avenue Matignon

The House of Heim is the oldest haute couture business in Paris still managed by members of the same family in direct descendency. Jacques Heim was noted for his eclectic collections featuring swimwear, furs, wedding, and débutante gowns. Before his death in 1967, he served as official dressmaker to Mme Charles de Gaulle. Today the fashion house is run by Philippe Jacques Heim, son of the founder.

21. Couture house of Marcel Rochas
14, avenue Matignon

By 1931, couturier Rochas was so successful that he resettled his business in this elegant mansion. Besides arranging the windows himself, he scoured the flea markets and antique shops for unusual objects to decorate his creations. In 1944, as a wedding gift to his third wife, he named his new perfume Femme and had it bottled in crystal Lalique flacons. After Rochas's death in 1954, the adored wife directed the Rochas perfume empire.

22. Couture house of Dessès
(17), avenue Matignon

In 1948 Dessès moved his maison de couture to the mansion that stood here and was formerly owned by the Eiffel family. Of Greek ancestry, Dessès originally came to Paris from Alexandria, Egypt, to study law and diplomacy. Instead, he filled his class notebooks with drawings of dresses, then sold them and began working for the Maison Jane before opening his own business in 1937.

23. Couture house of Callot Soeurs
9–11, avenue Matignon

The three Callot sisters moved their design house here in 1914. Mme Gerber, the oldest sister, was the major designer. By the late twenties, the house had passed into the hands of her son, Pierre Gerber, who produced quality at-home wear, pajamas, and tea gowns decorated with special fine laces. The designer Madeleine Vionnet, who trained at Callot Soeurs, wrote of the house: "Without the example of the Callot Soeurs, I would have continued to make Fords. It is because of them that I have been able to make Rolls Royces."

Turn left at the corner.

24. Henry James
42, avenue Gabriel

Miss Henrietta Reubell, a wealthy expatriate and friend of Henry James, lived here. His description of her as the character Miss Barrace in *The Ambassadors* (1903) reads: ". . . mature, meager, erect, and eminently gay, highly adorned, perfectly familiar, freely contradictious, and reminding him of some last-century portrait of a clever head without powder."

Walk on down the tree-lined avenue Gabriel to the United States embassy and you will pass the next two locations.

25. Formerly Les Ambassadeurs
(1), avenue Gabriel

Near the place de la Concorde end of the avenue is a theater owned by Pierre Cardin on the site of a former popular nightclub. In the Roaring Twenties, black American revues and jazz were the rage of Paris. *La revue nègre* started the trend. In 1926, a show from Harlem's Cotton Club played here and the Blackbirds— "the fifty copper colored girls"—comedians, and an orchestra delighted the audience. Black was beautiful and fashionable.

26. Residence of Coco Chanel and Arthur "Boy" Capel
Avenue Gabriel

Chanel often said that she had truly loved only once in her life—the man who seemed created for her—"Boy" Capel. He was "more than handsome," she said, "he was magnificent. He had a very strong, very individual personality, an ardent and concentrated nature." Capel initially financed Chanel in her own millinery business in 1910 and by the fall of that year Capel and Chanel shared an elegant apartment somewhere on the rue Gabriel. The year before he was killed in an automobile accident in 1919, Capel married Lady Wyndham and, according to Misia Sert, "Coco felt this loss so deeply that she sank into a neurasthenic state."

Now stroll back up the tree-shaded allée Marcel-Proust, next to the avenue des Champs-Elysées.

Another exclusive restaurant is still conducting business in the lush garden bordering the eastern half of the Champs-Elysées. Ledoyen, the interior décor in red velvet and white lace, was once a rural fresh dairy bar. The chestnut-tree-shaded terrace is the setting for James Tissot's 1885 painting, *The Artists' Wives.*

27. Short-term residence of John Steinbeck
1, avenue de Marigny

In the summer of 1954, John Steinbeck and his wife, Elaine, lived in this "pretty little house right in the center of Paris." He even suggested that his children play basketball in the courtyard which can be seen behind the high iron fence. The house had a roof terrace with flower boxes and a small study where Steinbeck worked. In a letter to Richard Rodgers and Oscar Hammerstein, he wrote that the house was "next to

Grand Palais and Petit Palais in the 1911 flood of the river Seine. (Courtesy of Duncan McElhone.)

the Rothschilds and across the street from the President of France. How's that for an address for a Salinas kid?"

Now, turn around and pass the park dominated by the Théâtre Marigny, cross the avenue des Champs-Elysées, and turn left on avenue Winston-Churchill. To your left are two important large museums, the Petit and the Grand Palais, built for the Universal Exhibition of 1900, the first world's fair to be held in Paris. The Petit Palais, Paris's municipal fine arts museum, houses an excellent collection of nineteenth-century paintings and is often the locale of temporary exhibitions. The large blockbuster exhibits and major retrospective shows are shown in the Grand Palais. It is an all-day project to visit these fine examples of Belle Epoque architecture.

After a right turn on the Cours la Reine, at the place du Canada, turn right.

28. Short-term residence of e. e. cummings
7, rue François-Ier, formerly Hôtel du Palais

Fresh from Harvard University, poet e. e. cummings volunteered in 1917 as a driver with the Norton-Hartjes Ambulance Corps in France. On board the troopship carrying him across the Atlantic, he met William Slater Brown, a graduate of the Columbia School of Journalism. Each evening they discussed literature and were still so busy talking as the boat train approached Paris, that when the commanding officer incorrectly ordered the troops to disembark, cummings and Brown did not hear the command. The rest of the detachment got off the train prematurely at a suburban station. The lucky twosome were the only ones to reach Paris and this hotel, the headquarters of the American volunteer forces. Now separated from their unit, the two young writers spent an idyllic month of May walking ten to twelve miles each day and attending the theater in the evening. Later recalling those days, cummings wrote: "Everywhere I sensed a miraculous presence, not of mere children and women and men, but of living human beings."

You will pass the dramatic modern building of Louis Vuitton, maker of the fine luggage which wealthy women of the Belle Epoque packed with haute couture gowns for travel to exotic destinations.

151

29. Subject of William Carlos Williams and headquarters of Pierre Cardin
Place François-Ier

Williams, an American doctor and poet, and his wife lived in Paris for six months in 1924. Retiring at three in the morning after a raucous party hosted by Robert McAlmon at the Trianon Restaurant on the Left Bank, Williams arose after a restless sleep to go out on a solitary walk. While eating a pear, he stumbled on the

> *medieval Place François Ier, as French in its way as anything I have ever known, of that French austerity of design, gray stone cleanly cut and put together in complementary masses, like the Alexandrines of Racine. . . . I saw a France that day which had wholly escaped me theretofore.*

The exquisite grey stone castle facing the square is headquarters for the Cardin empire that includes not only clothing but transportation, food (Maxim's), and communications.

Headquarters of the Pierre Cardin empire, place François-Ier. (Mary Ellen Jordan Haight.)

30. Residence of W. Somerset Maugham
(25), avenue Franklin-D.-Roosevelt

After his birth in the British Embassy, W. Somerset Maugham lived in the family home that formerly was here until his mother died, when he was sent to England for schooling. His early years in Paris remained fondly in his memory, and he often placed characters in his novels in the fashionable neighborhoods of the seventh, eighth, or sixteenth arrondissements. In *The Razor's Edge* (1944), Eliott Templeton warns about finding housing in the seventh: "Believe me, my dear fellow, the average American can get into the kingdom of heaven much more easily than he can get into the Boulevard Saint-Germain."

31. Formerly Bal Mabille
49–53, avenue Montaigne

By the middle of the nineteenth century, this neighborhood bar had grown into one of the largest and most popular dance halls in Paris. While watching the chorus line dance the cancan, accompanied by an orchestra of fifty musicians, the Civil War artist Winslow Homer observed a rose fall from a dancer's dress to the floor. Two sketches published in *Harper's* illustrate the frivolity down to the detail of the fallen flower. They were accompanied by the warning: "We shall not venture to look into the abyss on the brink of which these frenzied men and women are dancing. . . . This is work for the severe and steady eye of the preacher and moralist."

32. Couture house of Madeleine Vionnet
50, avenue Montaigne

Madeleine Vionnet moved her maison de couture in 1922 and she conducted her business at this location until she retired in 1939. Until her death in 1975 at the age of ninety-nine, she continued to be a commentator and critic on the high-fashion scene.

33. Couture house of Christian Dior
30–32, avenue Montaigne

Look for the ceramic plaque honoring Paul Poiret that is placed in the front sidewalk.

A former art dealer, Dior was described by Cecil Beaton as "a bland country curate, made out of pink marzipan." Dior opened his couture house in his favorite building in Paris, number thirty, in 1938 after apprenticeships with a few designers, including Lucien Lelong. The exterior and salons are still painted in shades of pearl-gray and white, with furnishings in Louis XVI style. Even today his panelled workroom and the old chairs are kept intact.

Dior created an international sensation in 1947 when he

Christian Dior. (Bibliothèque Nationale.)

unveiled the controversial "New Look." Susan Mary Alsop in her book, *To Marietta: Letters from Paris* (1975), describes her visit to Dior's salon:

> *It is impossible to exaggerate the prettiness of "The New Look." We are saved, becoming clothes are back, gone are the stern padded shoulders, in are the soft rounded shoulders without padding, nipped-in waists, wide, wide skirts about four inches below the knee. And such well-made armor inside the dress that one doesn't need underclothes.*

The billowing skirts were worn with picture hats and elbow-length gloves.

At the height of his success in 1957, at the age of fifty, Dior died suddenly of a stroke. He left an enormous empire, referred to by the *New York Times* as "the General Motors of the Paris haute couture." The company had divisions such as furs, perfumes, hats, shoes, and jewelry, and multiple foreign branches. Yves St. Laurent designed the brilliant 1958 Dior Trapeze collection the next year and was recognized as the successor to Dior's dominion.

34. Residence of Mary Cassatt
10, rue de Marignan

American impressionist painter Mary Cassatt lived here in a fifth-floor apartment from 1887 until her death in 1926. Her long residence in Paris began in 1868 when she came to study art and became a protégée and friend of Degas. In his book *L'art moderne* (1883), Oscar Wilde wrote of Cassatt's work shown at the impressionist exhibition of 1881: "Her works at the exhibition consist of portraits of children, also interiors, and they are a miracle. . . . She has succeeded in expressing . . . the joyful peace, the tranquil friendliness of the domestic interior."

35. Design house of Pierre Balmain
44, rue François-ler

Balmain was born in a small village in eastern France and, when war broke out in 1939, he left his job with Lucien Lelong in Paris to help his mother with her dress shop in Aix-les-Bains. It was here he first met Gertrude Stein and Alice B. Toklas, who were spending the war years in their summer home at Bilignin, not far from Aix. Stein wrote a friend that when their apparel became threadbare they were fortunate to meet a young man who made them each a suit of clothes. When their funds ran low in 1943, Stein sold her favorite Cézanne painting. Not long after the sale, Balmain, lunching with her, commented that the painting was no longer in its place on the dining room wall and asked what had become of it. "We are eating the Cézanne," she

Alice B. Toklas wearing a suit by Balmain. (Photo by Cecil Beaton, University Library, University of California at Los Angeles.)

told him without a trace of emotion. Stein and Toklas were once more at home in Paris in 1945 when Balmain opened his own design house. At the opening show, Stein whispered to photographer Cecil Beaton: "Don't tell anybody that we're wearing Pierre's clothes. We look too much like gypsies."

After Stein's death in 1946, Toklas continued the friendship with Balmain, who asked her to compose the introduction to the showing of his 1948 collection. Remarking on how unattractive and utilitarian much of twentieth-century fashion had been, she concluded: "Suddenly there was the awakening to the new understanding of what mode really was, the embellishment and the intensification of women's form and charm."

Backtrack one long, long block and turn left.

36. Théâtre des Champs-Elysées
13–15, avenue Montaigne

Constructed in 1913 as one of the first reinforced concrete buildings in Paris, the theater served as the city's main concert hall. The figure of American dancer Isadora Duncan can be seen carved in bas-relief by Antoine Bourdelle and in murals painted by Maurice Denis.

The opening in May 1918 featured the company of Diaghilev's Ballets Russes in the première performance of Claude Debussy's music to Mallarmé's "Afternoon of a Faun," with choreography by the principal dancer Vaslav Nijinsky. The cubist-inspired moves of the dancers distorted the angles and lines of traditional ballet, and Nijinsky scandalized the audience with his overtly severe and sensual performance. The shocked audience rioted and stamped their feet, shouting, "Call a dentist." How was a dentist supposed to repair the choreography?

On 20 June 1924, Diaghilev presented at this theater a truly collaborative experience between a painter, composer, choreographer, sculptor, couturière, and author-poet when *Le train bleu* opened to ecstatic reviews. The front curtain, designed by Picasso, was raised to reveal the sets, designed by sculptor Henri Laurens, and the dancers were costumed in uncomfortable wool bathing suits fashioned by Coco Chanel. Cocteau's scenario dealt with the young fashionable set frolicking on the côte d'Azur. The intricate gymnastics and acrobatics of the choreography by Bronislava Nijinska, sister of Nijinsky, were impossible for most dance companies to perform, and the work was not presented again until the Oakland California Ballet revived it in November 1989.

37. Short-term residence of Sinclair Lewis
2, avenue Montaigne, formerly Hôtel Elysées-Bellevue

Sinclair Lewis and his wife, Gracie, lived here for the winter of 1924–25 while he completed *Arrowsmith* (1925). Robert McAlmon, writer, and publisher of Contact Editions in the twenties, not only did not like Lewis personally, but thought his work not even second-rate. "He gives to the traveling salesman, the fake-superior pseudo-intellectual, and to the Europeans, a picture of America which they like to believe in order to feel their superiority."

From the rond point des Champs-Elysées with its beautiful fountains and bright flower gardens, it is a short walk to the Métro Champs-Elysées Clemenceau.

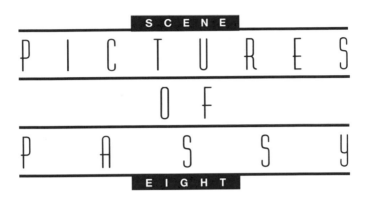

SCENE

PICTURES OF PASSY

EIGHT

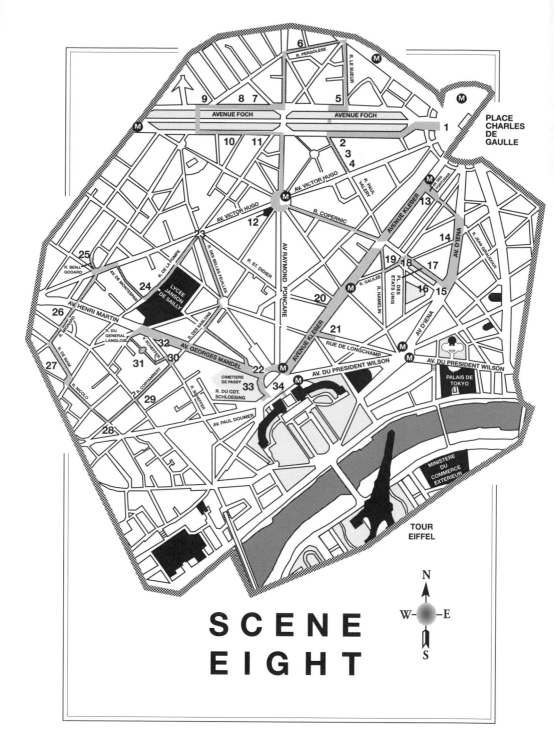

SCENE
EIGHT

"A perpetual garden party between the place Victor Hugo and the Seine" is Léon-Paul Fargue's description of Passy. The wide tree-lined avenues of suburban Passy, the quarter of old families and affluence, are in direct contrast to the narrow, winding, cobblestone streets of Montmartre. The eighteenth arrondissement of Scene One was home to the poor struggling artist, but Passy in the sixteenth arrondissement was where many successful artists and musicians resided. When Colette moved here in 1916, she wrote: "One is in flight from the crowds and the noise of the city." The few streets that are lined with small shops are referred to as the Village of Passy—the antithesis of a suburban shopping mall.

The atmosphere is that of a quiet village and, like a small town, it

> *is a large province in which the families know one another, keep an eye on one another—and sometimes hate one another, if one of them happens to have a few more guests, a few more politicians or poets than the other at his weekly, monthly, annual tea-party. . . . Pâtissiers, butchers, dry-cleaners and concierges know all about the family quarrels, divorces and inheritances. (Fargue, Le Piéton de Paris)*

Edgar Degas studied the crowds at Longchamps racecourse in the Bois de Boulogne and Emile Zola described the racing scene in *Nana* (1880). The former avenue Bois-de-Boulogne, now avenue Foch, was in the Victorian era the scene of a weekend parade of fashionably attired Parisians, including aristocratic *mondaines* (society) and *demimondaines* (courtesans) eyeing each other from elaborate carriages, or gossiping over dinner in one of the restaurants almost hidden in the verdant fields of the park. The Pré Catalan restaurant still serves expensive haute cuisine in an ancient pavilion surrounded by lush growth. No writer was more aware of the Bois's social charms than Proust, who wrote about it in *Du côté de chez Swann*, one of the thirteen volumes of his 1913–27 *A la recherche du temps perdu* (*Remembrances of Things Past*).

Métro Etoile Charles de Gaulle
Buses 92, 22, 30, 73, 52

Etoile (star) is an apt description of the wide streets radiating off the place Charles-de-Gaulle.

1. Viewing for Victor Hugo
Arc de Triomphe

Four years before he died, the broad avenue extending

southwest of the Arc de Triomphe in the sixteenth arrondissement was renamed for Victor Hugo to honor his eightieth year of vigor and literary excellence. In May 1885, his body lay in state for twenty-four hours atop a huge urn placed inside the arch. The solemn funeral procession the next day included every prominent French literary figure marching behind the cortège to the slow rhythm of dirges played by several brass bands. In Hugo's will he refused the prayers of all churches but stated that he believed in God. Therefore, by permission of the Catholic church, the Panthéon, which until that time had been a consecrated church building, was specially deconsecrated in order to accommodate Hugo's burial.

The funeral procession of Victor Hugo. (Bibliothèque Nationale.)

2. Residences of Henry Adams and Renée Vivian
23, avenue Foch

For several summers in the 1890s, Adams lived like a "twelfth-century monk in a nineteenth-century attic." Here he started his most monumental work, *Mont-Saint-Michel and Chartres* (1913) in which he noted the unity of the thirteenth century as symbolized by these memorials.

About ten years after Adams, the tragic young English poet Renée Vivian died prematurely from depression, drugs, and anorexia in an apartment here. Her near neighbor and close friend Colette, who had a life of some hardships but a strong will to survive, did not understand the frail heiress's obsession with death. On one of her visits to Renée's rooms, she was horrified to find the apartment darkened during the day, with pale candles burning in a dark velvet interior and a strong odor of lilies and incense clinging to the air. Vivian wrote sad poetry to Natalie Clifford Barney and her other lost female loves until her death in 1909, at not yet thirty-two years of age.

At the first corner, turn a hard left.

3. Residence of Sidonie-Gabrielle Colette
44, rue Paul-Valéry

Connected to Vivian's building by a courtyard and garden is the home Colette moved to in 1906, at the age of thirty-three, when she separated from the abusive husband who claimed authorship of her Claudine stories. She had been an innocent young native of Burgundy when, in 1893, she married Henri "Willy" Gauthier-Villars, the most powerful music critic in Paris. For thirteen years, he forced her to write the Claudine stories for sixteen hours a day shut in a dreary apartment. After finally leaving him and moving here to a ground-floor apartment, she supported herself by appearing on the stage. Her introduction to the Marquise de Belbeuf (Missy) resulted in a five-year period of lesbian attachments.

4. Residence of Berthe Morisot and Paul Valéry
40, rue Paul-Valéry

Impressionist artist Morisot's studio was the center of activity for many of the artistic and literary personalities of her day, particularly Manet and the other impressionists and author Stéphane Mallarmé. In 1874, she married Manet's brother Eugène. Berthe often painted her niece—who later married Paul Valéry—as a child and then as a young girl.

Morisot died in 1895, and in 1902 the Valérys occupied the apartment, which had walls covered with valuable paintings by Degas, Manet, Monet, Renoir, and, of course, Berthe Morisot herself.

In her book *Shakespeare and Company* (1956), Sylvia Beach tells of having lunch at the Valérys during the First World War. Just as they sat down to the table, an air-raid alert was sounded. "Valéry jumped up and rushed to the window and hung out to see the planes coming over Paris, dropping bombs. The family seemed accustomed to this behavior." His son François explained: "Papa adores these raids."

Retrace your steps across the wide park-lined avenue at the corner stoplight.

5. Residence of André Spire
34, avenue Foch

Imagine a sultry Sunday afternoon in 1920 in a second-floor apartment located in this stately, tree-shaded, four-story building. Look for the two sphinxes with women's heads guarding the entrances. Adrienne Monnier has invited Sylvia Beach, her close American friend and fellow bookshop proprietor of the rue de l'Odéon, to accompany her for supper at the home of French writer André Spire. Ezra Pound has brought James and Nora Joyce. Greeting Beach, Spire softly whispers in her ear: "The Irish writer James Joyce is here."

Beach worshipped Joyce and was so frightened she wanted to run away. It wasn't until after the cold supper that the fateful meeting took place, when Beach wandered into a little room lined to the ceiling with books. Upon seeing him, she asked: "Is this the great James Joyce?" After responding "James Joyce," he shook hands with her. Beach later wrote: "That is, he put his limp, boneless hand in my tough little paw— if you can call that a handshake." She saw a light of genius shining in Joyce's "deep beautiful eyes." From this first impression, she was always conscious of his genius, "yet I knew no one so easy to talk to."

6. Short-term residence of F. Scott and Zelda Fitzgerald
10, rue Pergolèse

After an unpleasant summer on the Riviera, during which Scott quarreled with their affable friends, the Gerald Murphys, the Fitzgeralds stayed here during the fall of 1929.

It had been almost ten years since their marriage—years of flight from responsibility, drunkenness, pranks that annoyed their friends, and conflict with each other. Zelda, spending whole days in ballet practice, was losing weight, and friends reported that she appeared withdrawn into her private world. The winter and the spring months of 1930 passed with eccentric behavior by Zelda and little writing by Scott; he was working on *Tender Is the Night* (1934) and wrote to his editor, Max Perkins, of his inability to focus on the project.

At the end of April, Zelda was hospitalized for a mental breakdown. After a diagnosis of schizophrenia, she spent most of the next year and a half in a hospital near Geneva, Switzerland, and Scott gave up this apartment to live near the sanitarium.

7. Residence of Misia and Thadée Natanson
60, avenue Foch

The Natansons gave a party in 1895 to show off their sumptuous new home to three hundred friends. The party—and the house—were the talk of Paris. Decorating the dining room were nine large decorative panels by Vuillard depicting women and children frolicking in a public garden. For the gala evening, Toulouse-Lautrec—all four and a half feet of him, dressed in white, with a waistcoat made from an American flag—had shaved his head. Serving as a bartender, he concocted unimagined drinks of ghastly bright green, red, and yellow liqueurs, some of which he set aflame. Before long, the victims of his mad inventions were clinging to the bar with one hand while clutching their drinks with the other. By dawn, Toulouse-Lautrec proudly announced that he had served two thousand drinks and had succeeded in getting everyone drunk while he, for possibly the first time, remained completely sober.

8. Residence of James Tissot
64, avenue Foch

In 1867, Tissot purchased the house he occupied until his death in 1902. His work is divided into two sections—his pre- and post-religious-conversion periods. Until 1895, there were paintings of elegantly dressed, beautiful young women representative of London and Paris society. After his conversion, he produced huge numbers of Old Testament theme paintings—as many as 350 watercolors in one year.

9. Residence of Anatole France
72, avenue Foch

Janet Flanner, "Genêt," in 1925 described France's funeral as

J. J. J. Tissot, The Artists' Wives, *1885, on the terrace of Ledoyen's restaurant on the avenue Champs-Elysées. (The Chrysler Museum, gift of Walter P. Chrysler, Jr., and Grandy Fund, Landmark Communications Fund and "An Affair to Remember" 1982.)*

"one of the biggest, most pretentious spectacles modern Paris has ever seen. . . . Victor Hugo's famous cortège was a family affair beside the thousands that followed France." Jacques Anatole Thault, "Anatole France," the son of a book dealer, resided here and died in 1924 at the age of eighty. Three years previously he had been awarded the Nobel Prize in Literature for his political satire *La révolte des anges* (1914) (*Revolt of Angels*). According to Flanner, after his death he was more popular in the United States than in his native France.

Go back to the other side of the avenue and stop at the corner of rue Picot.

10. Residence of Pauline Pfeiffer
Rue Picot

Prior to becoming the second Mrs. Ernest Hemingway, Pauline Pfeiffer came to Paris from the Midwest to work as assistant to Mainbocher, the European editor of *Vogue* magazine. Upon meeting Ernest and Hadley Hemingway in 1925, she was soon a "friend of the family" and in love with Ernest. In February 1926, after a fling with Ernest alone in Paris, Pauline wrote to Hadley, who was waiting for her husband to return to their winter residence in Schruns, Austria: "Your husband, Ernest, was a delight to me. I tried to see him as much as he could see me and was possible."

Backtrack to the place Venezuela.

11. Residence of Archibald MacLeish
41, avenue Foch

This magnificent building was the residence of Archibald and Ada MacLeish for about a year between 1926 and 1927. It was not that the couple had the great wealth it would take to live here. Their good friend, Pierpont Morgan Hamilton, great-great-grandson of Alexander Hamilton and nephew of J. Pierpont Morgan, wished to keep his staff of eight employed during his absence, so he asked the MacLeishes to occupy the apartment in exchange for just payment of the staff salaries. The twelve rooms included a grand salon measuring sixty by thirty feet. Sylvia Beach recalled dining here with the Joyces and Adrienne Monnier; after dinner Archie read a partly finished poem and Ada sang in a beautiful voice.

MacLeish was graduated from Yale University and Harvard

Law School, but in 1923 he abandoned the practice of law to write poetry and would eventually be granted three Nobel Prizes in literature. In 1932 he sent his long poem, *Conquistador* (later to win a Pulitzer Prize), to Ezra Pound, who announced that it was "damned bad." Another friend, Ernest Hemingway, in 1945, expressed similar feelings about MacLeish's work: "Does Archie still write anything except Patriotic? I read some awfully lifeless lines to a Dead Soldier by him in that Free World anthology."

Turn right down avenue Raymond-Poincaré.

12. Marriage site of Ernest and Pauline Hemingway
9, place Victor-Hugo, Eglise Saint-Honoré-d'Eylou

On 10 May 1927 Hemingway married Pfeiffer here in a Catholic ceremony; he claimed to have been baptized on a battleground in Italy during World War I. The bride, her black hair bobbed and combed across her forehead, wore a creamy silk dress accented by a single strand of pearls. The groom wore a three-piece tweed suit, button-down collared shirt, and a dark tie. The couple honeymooned in a small fishing village at the mouth of the Rhône River estuary.

From the square, go east on rue Copernic and left at avenue Kléber.

13. Short-term residence of George Gershwin
19, avenue Kléber, formerly Hôtel Majestic

A newspaper ad in 1906 described the hotel as "located in the most fashionable and healthiest part of the city, 400 bedrooms and salons, 200 private baths, central heating. Concerts every evening and a large roof garden." It is now the Centre de Conférences Internationales.

George Gershwin occupied a suite in 1928 while composing *An American in Paris:* "My purpose here is to portray the impression of an American visitor in Paris as he strolls through the city, and listens to various street noises and absorbs the French atmosphere." On the piano in his room, Gershwin played for fellow musicians Darius Milhaud, Prokofiev, Cole Porter, William Walton, and Leopold Stokowski.

Walk right at Etoile to the second street and turn right at avenue d'Iéna and proceed to rue Galilée.

14. Residence of James Joyce
Rue Galilée

Joyce always lived beyond his income, and his admirers often provided the means. Sylvia Beach, the first publisher of *Ulysses*, advanced money for ten years to cover the Joyce family living expenses. She made no direct profit from sales of the book. When Random House purchased the book in 1932, Joyce did not repay her nor give her proper credit; as Beach said, "He has not only robbed me, but taken away my character." In 1933, until the lease ran out in the summer of 1934, James and Nora and their adult daughter, Lucia, lived in a drably furnished, impersonal apartment somewhere on this street in this good neighborhood. They were often patrons of the opera; James dressed in a silk-lined evening cape, wearing a silk top hat and carrying an iron-tipped cane, and Nora wore the latest fashion from Lucien Lelong. Hers was not an easy life with this egotistical, eccentric genius and their schizophrenic daughter, so clothes became an emotional outlet. Once, when apologizing after a domestic quarrel in front of Bennett Cerf, Nora laughingly said: "Sometime I'm going to write a book and I'm going to call it 'My Twenty Years with Genius—So Called.'"

15. Short-term residence of Charles Lindbergh
(2), avenue d'Iéna, formerly the American ambassador's private residence

The building at the end of the avenue overlooking the Eiffel Tower no longer exists, so imagine going there on 24 May 1927, when 150,000 people jammed the access road and the airport at Le Bourget outside Paris, screaming "Lind-ee, Lind-ee!" As Charles A. Lindbergh stepped from his small monoplane he remarked: "Am I here? Is this really Paris?" He had been forty hours without sleep. Josephine Baker interrupted her performance at the Folies Bergères to announce the news of his arrival. He was whisked from the airport to this residence, which Ambassador Myron T. Herrick purchased with his own money. After a welcome bath and meal of bouillon, poached egg, and milk, an excited Lindy slept a few hours, attired in silk pajamas belonging to the ambassador. The next day at a press conference at the American Embassy, Lindbergh's unassuming modesty and clean-cut youthful good looks, combined with his daring exploit, made him the most celebrated American in Paris of all time. For the next week, Lindbergh stayed here and joined in the celebrations that climaxed with an official reception at the Hôtel de Ville (city hall) before a square packed with forty thousand people.

Follow the avenue toward the river.

16. Residence of Edith Wharton
3, place des Etats-Unis

Wharton escaped the life of an upper-class wealthy matron by becoming a successful writer, and she managed to flee the "unenlightened ugliness" (as described by her friend Henry James) of upper-class New York by moving to Paris in the winter of 1905 and living in a Right Bank hotel. In mid-April 1906, her brother, Harry Jones, invited her to move into his townhouse overlooking the small, quiet square. She was beginning to love "the steady nourishment of the warm dim background of a long social past" that Paris offered. With her husband, Teddy, she went on to England and then back home to New England, but she returned to Paris in January 1907, the year her acclaimed novel *House of Mirth* was published. Wharton lived in France until her death in 1937.

17. Short-term residence of Gloria Swanson
10, place des Etats-Unis

Prior to World War I the French led the world's film industry, but it was in shambles after the war and Hollywood took the lead. By the twenties, the French were in love with American movies and movie stars, and Samuel Putnam wrote that "young French men were to be seen imitating the slick-back hair and flaring-bottomed trousers of Rudolph Valentino while the girls did their best to imitate the mannerisms of Gloria Swanson."

The glamorous Miss Swanson lived here while filming *Madame Sans-Gêne* during October and November 1928. The bedroom in her third-floor apartment was lacquered in black and had a gold bed in one corner and a sunken Roman bath in the other. After visiting Swanson—and presumably her bedroom—a movie studio executive cabled Cecil B. DeMille: "You are right after all! These things actually exist outside of your studio."

18. Place des Etats-Unis

Now is a good time to rest on one of the park benches near the memorial to President George Washington and the French general Lafayette, who served in the colonial army during the

American Revolution. Bertholdi sculpted the work after completing the Statue of Liberty, and it was presented to the city of Paris by newspaper mogul Joseph Pulitzer at a huge unveiling ceremony on 4 July 1900. The American and French anthems were played by the new sixty-three-member band of John Philip Sousa. His aim in signing up European musicians to play with him was "to make this band equal in executive ability to the band of the *Garde républicaine* in Paris"; it was the first American band to parade through the streets of Paris escorted by the horse-mounted Garde républicaine. In the 1989 celebration of the bicentennial of the French Republic, the mayor of Paris inaugurated the extensively renovated gardens, followed by a long parade of fifty marching bands from the United

Monument to George Washington and the marquis de Lafayette in the place des Etats-Unis. (Mary Ellen Jordan Haight.)

171

States in front of the Hôtel de Ville, which was gaily decorated with hundreds of stars and stripes. A pouring rain did not dampen American Day in Paris as thousands of French and Americans together sang the "Marseillaise" and "The Star-Spangled Banner."

Exit the square by turning left on rue Galilée, and then take a right turn at the next corner.

19. Site of Marcel Proust's death
44, rue Hamelin, Hôtel Union Etoile

The plaque over the entrance denotes the location of Proust's death on 18 November 1922—in a sparsely furnished room with only a reproduction of Whistler's *Carlyle* on the walls. Two days after his death, at the request of his brother Dr. Robert Proust, the American surrealist Man Ray photographed Proust's folded hands and his head.

On New Year's Eve 1921, Proust was expected at a party hosted by Etienne de Beaumont, who announced to his gathered guests that Proust's housekeeper had telephoned for the tenth time wanting to know if the house was drafty and if the herb tea for Proust was ready.

> *Finally at midnight there was a kind of stir in the crowd and we knew that Proust was there. He had entered with the New Year, the year of his death. . . . His pale face had become puffy; he had developed a paunch. He spoke only to dukes.*

"Look at him," Picasso said, "he's pursuing his theme."

Proust's semiautobiographical sixteen-volume cyclic novel, *Remembrance of Things Past*, written between 1913 and 1927, is considered by many to be the greatest French novel of the twentieth century.

At the next corner, turn right on rue Boissière, then left on avenue Kléber and right at the second street.

20. Residence of Ludwig Lewisohn
12, rue Saint-Didier

In 1925, the German-born American ex-journalist and teacher fled from his ex-wife thinking he could find sympathetic friends in Paris. Finding he had nothing in common with the other American expatriates, except on the "ground of mere human friendliness," he wrote as many as a thousand words a day to document his unhappy marriage. In four and a half months, he shipped the completed

150,000-word manuscript to his American publisher, Horace Liveright, who thought it was clearly libelous and declined to publish it. Edward Titus, husband of cosmetic tycoon Helena Rubenstein, then published the book at his Black Manikin Press under the title, *The Case of Mr. Crump* (1925). Lewisohn declared his moral satisfaction and anticipated a large American sale. The book Lewisohn called a work of the "severest moral idealism" was blacklisted by the United States Post Office on the grounds that it violated the same criminal code that had denied James Joyce's *Ulysses* entry into America. *Crump* did bear the dubious distinction of being the first of three books published by Titus to go out of print.

At the next corner, avenue Raymond-Poincaré, take a left for two blocks.

21. Residence of Stephen Vincent Benét
36, rue de Longchamp

Benét moved into a building formerly located here in the summer of 1927, while working on his Pulitzer Prize–winning poem *John Brown's Body* (1919). His small fifth-floor room had tiny porthole windows that on cold days let out all of the heat generated by the humble stove. By November he told a friend: "I was swearing at John Brown's damn body whenever I had a minute, trying to get it off."

When Sylvia Beach opened her bookshop in 1921, Benét was one of the first customers. At his request, and "on his own responsibility," she took him to meet Gertrude Stein.

> *The visit to Gertrude went off pleasantly. I believe Stephen mentioned that he had some Spanish blood, and since Gertrude and Alice liked anything Spanish, that interested them. I don't think the meeting left any traces, however.*

At the large, busy place du Trocadéro, turn right, then right again onto rue Greuze.

22. Residence of Gerald and Sara Murphy
2, rue Greuze

Charming and elegant Gerald Murphy and his family arrived in Paris in the fall of 1921. After a short stay at a hotel, they settled in this building. Not wanting to work in the family leather business, Mark Cross, Gerald had studied landscape architecture at Harvard University, and then, to escape family pressures and for cultural enrichment, moved his young family to Europe. The trend-setting couple was the subject of Calvin Tomkins's *Living Well Is the Best Revenge* (1962).

Soon after his arrival, Gerald saw the modernist paintings by Braque, Picasso, and Juan Gris.

> *I was astounded. My reaction to the color and form was immediate. To me there was something in these paintings that was instantly sympathetic and comprehensible. I remember saying to Sara, 'If that's painting, it's what I want to do.'*

Murphy painted for nine years and produced ten amazing canvasses that are reminiscent of American pop art.

Continue and turn right at the corner to the place de Mexico.

23. Residence of Harry and Caresse Crosby
40, rue des Belles-Feuilles

Another well-off young American couple, the Crosbys, arrived in Paris in the fall of 1922 as newlyweds with two children from Polly's (she had not yet adopted her new first name) first marriage to Boston socialite Richard Peabody. Because Harry felt he had married a mistress, not a mother, he refused to accept Polly's maternal role.

At this first Paris residence the children were kept virtual prisoners in their nursery. When the maid changed the linen in the master bedroom twice a week, Polly allowed them to jump up and down on the bed, an activity the children regarded as the high spot of their week.

At the corner of avenue Victor Hugo, turn left and then take again an immediate left. Turn right at number 99 into the tiny lane which is avenue de Montespan.

24. Residence of Isadora Duncan
99, rue de la Pompe, and 9, avenue de Montespan

Isadora Duncan bought the former Salle Beethoven in 1919. In her *New Yorker* column, Janet Flanner wrote that Duncan's Sunday night suppers were

> *banquets where guests strolled in, strolled out, and from low divans supped principally on champagne and strawberry tarts, while Isadora, barely clad in chiffon robes, rose when the spirit moved her to dance exquisitely. Week after week came obscure people whose names she never even knew. They were like moths. She once gave a house party that started in Paris,*

gathered force in Venice, and culminated weeks later on a houseboat on the Nile.

She left the house in 1921 to open a school of dance in Moscow.

Continue on the cobblestone street to avenue Victor Hugo, turn left for a short block, then right.

25. Short-term residence of Edna St. Vincent Millay
5, rue Benjamin-Godard

During the month of June 1932, Millay lived at this address. She had just published *Fatal Interview*, a sonnet cycle in the Elizabethan manner. Her short visits to France did not result in an ability to speak the language, nor did she associate much with the people.

Backtrack and cross avenue Victor Hugo to the opposite side of square Lamartine.

26. Birthplace of Jean-Paul Sartre
2, rue Mignard

Existentialist philosopher Sartre was born in June 1905 in this building on the corner of rue de Siam. Because his father, a naval officer, was frequently absent, Sartre and his mother lived with her parents. Just about fifteen months after his birth, Sartre's father died; and for the next ten years, until his mother remarried, he was raised by his grandparents. The young Jean-Paul was educated at the most prestigious schools in Paris, the Lycée Henry IV and the Ecole Normale Supérieure.

When Sartre's autobiograpical masterpiece, *The Words* (1963) was awarded the 1964 Nobel Prize, he refused to accept the honor, saying, "I have always declined official distinctions. The writer must refuse to let himself be transformed by institutions, even if these are of the most honorable kind, as is the case here." In Europe and throughout the world, Sartre became the symbol of the engaged intellectual, a thinker who tried seriously to be involved in the realities that surrounded him.

27. Residence of George Gïssing
13, rue de Siam

The late nineteenth-century English novelist Gïssing was influenced by Charles Dickens and the French naturalist movement in literature represented by Gustave Flaubert, Guy de Maupassant,

Zola, and the Goncourt brothers. Gïssing's desire for scientific objectivity gave a sharp focus to his descriptive writing. Working-class life on the streets of Paris was never described better. In 1903, the year of his death, he wrote the semiautobiographical *Private Paper of Henry Ryecroft.*

Cross rue de la Pompe and on rue Nicolo turn left at the second block.

28. Residence of Colette
57, rue Cortambert

With her second husband, Henry de Jouvenel, Colette lived in an old wooden chalet in 1911. He was the editor of the Paris newspaper *Le Matin* and led a life of magnificence. Colette had been performing in music halls for five years, but with her marriage and pregnancy she retired from the stage. At the age of forty, Colette gave birth to her only child, a daughter, Colette, known as Bel-Gazou.

The year 1913 saw the publication of *L'envers du music-hall* (*Backstage of the Music Hall*), Colette's nostalgic sketches and vignettes of backstage life as she had experienced it. The book is distinctly different from her Claudine books.

Turn right at the next block.

29. Residence of Emmanuel Frémiet
70, rue de la Tour

The most celebrated sculptor of animals in the later nineteenth century, Frémiet began his career as painter at the Paris morgue. He studied animals in the Jardin des Plantes, where, in 1890, his *Stone Age Man* was installed. Probably his most curious commission came from Napoléon III, who requested fifty-five statuettes exhibiting all the uniforms of the army.

Retrace your steps and continue on rue Cortambert to the next corner.

30. Residence of Comtesse Anne de Noailles
40, rue Scheffer

This is a fine example of a magnificent *hôtel particulier,* or private mansion, of the eighteenth century. The Countess de Noailles, daughter of a Rumanian prince and a Greek mother, moved here in 1910 and stayed until her death on 30 April 1933. At their first meeting in 1906, Edith Wharton was moved by the countess's beautiful looks, her dark hair cut low on her forehead, her deep melancholy eyes, and her sensuous lips. According to Wharton, she was "quite exceptionally interesting," picturesque and fanciful, brilliant in conversation, and "like a little exotic bird."

It was in her bedroom with walls papered in a soft yellow-and-blue chintz pattern that she received friends while lying in a bed covered in lemon-yellow satin. Two volumes of poetry and three short novels, each exploring the psychology of women in love, were authored by de Noailles. She was the first woman to be received into the Académie royale de langue et de littérature françaises de Belgique and, after her death, the honor was bestowed on her good friend Colette. Describing their first meeting, Colette wrote:

> *At this time, when her beauty was that of an adolescent, the world was already flocking to her; she accepted homage with the majesty and gravity of a child, and she seemed neither profoundly happy, nor intoxicated, for nothing human cures the melancholy of the elect.*

The bedroom of Comtesse Anne de Noailles, poet and arts patron. (Musées de la Ville de Paris by SPADEM 198.)

Turn into the villa Scheffer and walk up the curving small street to number 17.

31. Residence of George and Helen Joyce
17, villa Scheffer

James and Nora Joyce's only son and his American wife, Helen, returned from New York in September 1936 to live in this grand, spacious flat with French doors leading onto a garden. Besides their small son, Stephen, the household included a cook, a chauffeur, and a dog. At the age of thirty-one, after failing at a singing career, George was living off his wife's wealth. He did spend three days working with Samuel Beckett reading the difficult proofs of the galleys of his father's *Work in Progress*. As usual, George was unpaid by his father. Beckett would also have worked without remuneration, but out of politeness accepted the 250 francs, a used overcoat, and five worn neckties offered by Joyce.

In 1937, James and Nora took George, Helen, Beckett, and Helen's friend Peggy Guggenheim to dinner, following which they all returned to this house. Beckett, entranced with Peggy, stared at her and asked to accompany her home; after a twenty-four-hour love affair, Beckett thanked her and said, "It was nice while it lasted."

Continue through villa Scheffer and rue du Général-Langlois, then turn right for a short block, then right again.

32. Residence of Winnaretta Singer de Polignac
43, avenue Georges-Mandel

The daughter of the inventor of the Singer sewing machine was raised in France, and at twenty-eight she married the much older Prince Edmond de Polignac, an uncle of Prince Pierre de Monaco (father of Prince Rainier). As a surprise Christmas present in 1900, she presented to her husband a famous small palace on the Grand Canal in Venice, but he died not long after. She used her considerable fortune to fund many of the arts and, due to an intense interest in ballet, she financed many of Diaghilev's Ballets Russes. It was her influence in Monaco that allowed the Ballets to spend six months of each year in Monte Carlo as their permanent home. Igor Stravinsky said of the princess that she was "immensely cultivated, an excellent musician and a painter endowed with undoubtable talent."

Princesse de Polignac purchased this magnificent mansion in

Winnaretta Singer (Princess Edmond de Polignac), of the influential Singer sewing machine family. (Bibliothèque Nationale.)

1890, and many famous musicians performed in the eighteenth-century mirror-lined music room. Her commissioned works by Stravinsky, Ravel, and Milhaud were premièred here. In 1927 Stravinsky and Prokofiev played duets before Americans Henry James, Isadora Duncan, Cole Porter, and Ezra Pound. Included in her fine art collection were works by Monet, Manet, and Renoir.

The Singer-Polignac Foundation administration offices, established here on 28 March 1928, provide scholarships to students of art and music. Concerts are still held in the music room.

Return to rue Scheffer and turn left at rue Petrarque, then onto rue du Compte-Schloesing.

33. Cimetière de Passy
Rue du Compte-Schloesing

The most famous tombs in this cemetery belong to Debussy, Manet, and Morisot. Just off the center circle, under a bust of Edouard Manet, are the graves of his wife, Suzanne Leenhoff; his brother, Eugène Manet; and Eugène's wife, painter Berthe Morisot.

Edouard Manet died in Paris in 1893, at the age of fifty-one. Two of his paintings had been accepted by the conservative judges of the

1861 salon, but two years later his now-famous painting of two nude women sitting in the bois with two fully clothed men, *Le déjeuner sur l'herbe*, was rejected by the critics as obscene. Manet refused to exhibit with the impressionists, yet reviewers condemned his canvasses as works "for which no words are too bad." This made him the most celebrated painter in Paris, but not in the way he had desired.

Morisot's lighter impressionistic work was readily accepted into the salon exhibits. Her work employed subtle colors and white on white with a linear look. Morisot converted Manet—who was schooled to paint outdoor scenes in the studio—to the impressionist's joy of painting in the open air with the natural light and scenery.

In a section of the cemetery toward avenue Georges-Mendel are buried the composers Gabriel Fauré and Claude Debussy. Teacher and organist Fauré greatly influenced the compositions of Debussy. In 1905 he became the director of the Paris Conservatoire, and until his death in 1924, he willingly shared his time and advice with the musicians of the younger generation.

Debussy is buried in a black tomb with his name etched in gold. The innovative impressionistic composer is now believed to have laid the foundation for much of twentieth-century music. He felt that music should reflect emotion and that the dramatic arias of opera were unnatural and false. When he died in 1918, his hearse was followed to this cemetery by only a small group of his remaining friends, echoing his independent life of aloofness and preference for the company of his Angora cats.

The charming small house in which Honoré de Balzac lived for five and a half years, beginning in September 1841, is just a little too far off the path to include in this walk. It is now the Musée Balzac (47, rue Raynouard) and is worth a visit. Here Balzac wrote some of his finest novels by following a strenuous routine: rising at midnight, working for eight hours, spending fifteen minutes eating a meal, working again until five in the afternoon, dining, then sleeping six hours.

34. Tour Eiffel
Place du Trocadéro et du 11 Novembre

Cross the place du Trocadéro et du 11 Novembre to the Palais de Chaillot. The existing twin buildings were constructed in 1937 for the Paris Exhibition, replacing the former Palais du Trocadéro, erected for the earlier 1878 Exhibition. From the terrace you can view the only landmark in this book that is situated across the River Seine on the Left Bank.

Former Trocadéro about 1910. (From Paris Illustrated, *courtesy of Thomas Gee.)*

At the time Gustave Eiffel's architectural miracle was opened for the Exposition Universelle in 1889, his "work of uselessness" unleashed a passionate debate. A group of intellectuals, including the novelists Guy de Maupassant and Alexandre Dumas, signed a petition "protesting against this ridiculous chimney erected to the glory of the vandalism of industrial enterprises." Totally unconcerned, Eiffel stated that "when it's finished, they will love it." At the beginning of the twentieth century, the tower was threatened with destruction until a new use was found for it as the perfect location for a radio aerial. During the past 101 years, more than 125 million persons have visited what poet Guillaume Apollinaire called the "shepherdess of the clouds." For the centennial celebration in 1989, there gleamed from the top a brilliant star that changed slowly from red to white, from white to blue, and from blue to red in a continuous cycle. The letters "100 *ans* [years]" ran its length. A $10-million party replete with a 76-foot-tall birthday cake baked by 1,000 chefs, and a show complete with 3,500 extras, 300 fashion models, 100 accordionists, and 20 international entertainers topped the celebration.

Guy de Maupassant frequently lunched in the restaurant in the top of the tower, though he did not really care much for the food. About the tower, he wrote: "It's the only place in Paris where I don't have to see it." The French cultural critic Roland Barthes described the effect the tower has on visitors:

Completion of the Eiffel Tower as the centerpiece of the 1889 International Exhibition of Paris. (La Réunion des Musées Nationaux.)

It has the illusion of raising the enormous lid which covers the private lives of millions of human beings; the city then becomes an intimacy whose functions, i.e., whose connections he deciphers; on the great polar axis, perpendicular to the horizontal curve of the river, three zones stacked one after the other, as though along a prone body, three functions of human life: at the top, at the foot of Montmartre, pleasure; at the centre, around the Opera, materiality, business, commerce; towards the bottom, at the foot of the Panthéon, knowledge, study; then, to the right and left, enveloping this vital axis like two protective muffs, two large zones of habitation, one residential, the other blue-collar; still farther, two wooded, Boulogne and Vincennes ....

As Bill Gorton said of Paris, in Hemingway's *The Sun Also Rises*, "It's pretty grand," and "I love to get back."

BIBLIOGRAPHY

"A Renoir is Sold for $78 million." *San Francisco Chronicle*. 18 May 1990.

"A $38.46 Million Picasso." *San Francisco Chronicle*. 29 Nov. 1988.

Adhémar, Hélène, and Jean Adhémar, eds. *Chronologie impressionniste*. Paris: Editions de la Réunion des musées nationaux, 1981.

Aillaud, C. "A Lanvin Legacy: Establishing a Family Tradition in Paris." *Architectural Digest*, Sept. 1988.

Allan, Tony. *The Glamour Years Paris 1919–1940*. New York: W. H. Smith, 1977.

Alsop, Susan Mary. "Pei's Pyramid—New Jewel of the Seine." *Architectural Digest*, April 1989.

Anderson, Chester C. *James Joyce and His World*. London: Peter Owen, 1966.

Anonymous. *The Shuttered Houses of Paris*. New York: Grove Press, Inc., 1986.

Arminjon, Catherine, *et al. L'Art de Vivre*. New York: The Vendome Press, 1989.

Baer, Nancy Van Norman. "The Art of Enchantment: Diaghilev's Ballets Russes, 1909–1929." *Triptych*. San Francisco: The Museum Society, Nov., Dec. and Jan. 1988.

Bair, Deirdre. "Colette: Homes of the Heart." *New York Times Magazine*, 1 Oct. 1989.

Baker, Kenneth. "Degas: A Retrospective." *San Francisco Chronicle*, 26 June 1988.

Baker, Kenneth. "Subtle Shadows." *San Francisco Examiner Review*, Aug. 1988.

Balenciaga: The Art and the Skill." *International Herald Tribune*, 1 Aug. 1989.

Beach, Sylvia. *Shakespeare and Company*. Lincoln: University of Nebraska Press, 1959.

Behbehani, Mandy. "Dressed for Debate." *San Francisco Examiner*, 28 May 1989.

Benstock, Shari. *Women of the Left Bank*. Austin: University of Texas Press, 1986.

Bertrand, Jules. *Paris 1870–1945*. London: Sampson Low, Marston, 1946.

Blume, Mary. "American in Paris." *Our Century Our World*. Paris: *International Herald Tribune*, Feb. 1987.

Blume, Mary. "Coco Chanel Revisited." *Architectural Digest*, Sept. 1988.

Blume, Mary. "The Passages of Paris." *International Herald Tribune*, 8 May 1989.

Brassai. *Picasso and Company*. New York: Doubleday and Co., 1977.

Brinnon, John Malcolm. *Sextette*. New York: Dell, 1981.

Brody, Elaine. *Paris: The Musical Kaleidoscope 1870–1925*. New York: George Braziller, 1987.

Buchwald, Art. *Art Buchwald, Paris*. Boston: Little, Brown, 1952.

Burnett, Avis. *Gertrude Stein*. New York: Atheneum, 1972.

Cabanne, Pierre. *Picasso His Life and Times*. New York: William Morrow and Co., 1977.

Calvert, George H. *Scenes and Thoughts in Europe*. New York: G. P. Putnam, 1855.

Charles-Roux, Edmonde. *Chanel and Her World*. New York: Vendome Press, 1979.

Copland, Aaron, and Vivian Perlès. *Copland 1900–1942*. New York: St. Martins/Marek, 1984.

Corrigan, Patricia. "A Dancer's Light Touch, La Belle Américaine." *St. Louis Post Dispatch*, 1 Nov. 1987.

Coughlon, Robert. *The Wine of Genius—Utrillo*. New York: Harper, 1951.

Culbertson, Judi, and Tom Randall. *Permanent Parisians*. Chelsea, VT: Chelsea Green, 1986.

Cummings, e. e. "is 5, two, IX," *Poems 1923–54*. New York: Harcourt, Brace, 1954.

Denvir, Bernard, ed. *The Impressionists at First Hand*. London: Thames and Hudson, Ltd., 1987.

Donnally, Trish. "A Rich Trove of Costumes for the Ballet." *San Francisco Chronicle*, 1 Dec. 1988.

Donnally, Trish. "It's Coco's Kind of Boutique." *San Francisco Chronicle*, 22 Nov. 1988.

"Excess of Revelry." *San Francisco Chronicle*. 17 June 1989.

Fields, Armond. *George Auriol*. Salt

Lake City: Gibbs M. Smith, 1985.

Figes, Eva. *Light*. New York: Ballantine, 1983.

"The Finery of a Royal Mistress." *International Herald Tribune*. 6 and 7 May 1989.

Fisher, M. F. K. *As They Were*. New York: Knopf, 1989.

Fitzgerald, F. Scott. *Correspondence of F. Scott Fitzgerald*. Edited by Matthew J. Bruccoli and Margaret M. Duggan. New York: Random House, 1980.

Flanner, Janet. *An American in Paris*. London: Hamish Hamilton, 1940.

Flanner, Janet. *Paris Was Yesterday*. London: Angus and Robertson, 1973.

Ford, Hugh. *Published in Paris*. New York: The Pushcart Press, 1980.

Fox, Milton S., ed. *Utrillo*. New York: Harry N. Abrams, 1953.

Gibbs, Philip. *European Journey*. New York: Literary Guild, 1934.

Gibbings, Robert. *Coming Down the Seine*. London: J. M. Dent and Sons, 1955.

Glimcher, Arnold, and Marc Glimcher, eds. *Je suis le cahier*. Boston/ New York: Atlantic Monthly Press, 1986.

Gold, Arthur, and Robert Fizdale. *Misia*. New York: Morrow Quill Paperbacks, 1981.

Guggenheim, Peggy. *Out of this Century*. London: André Deutsch Ltd., 1987.

Haight, Mary Ellen Jordan. *Walks in Gertrude Stein's Paris*. Salt Lake City: Gibbs M. Smith, 1988.

Halpern, Daniel, ed. *Writers on Artists*. San Francisco: North Point Press, 1988.

Harris, Dale. "Legends: Chanel and Diaghilev." *Architectural Digest,* Sept. 1989.

Harris, Dale. "The Opulent Era." *Architectural Digest,* Sept. 1989.

Heilbrun, François, and Philippe Néagu. *Portraits d'artistes*. Paris: Editions de la Réunion des musées nationaux, 1986.

Hemming, F. W. *Culture and Society in France 1849–1898*. New York: Scribner, 1900.

Hemingway, Ernest. *The Sun Also Rises*. New York: Charles Scribner's Sons, 1926.

Hemingway, Ernest. "My Old Man." *The Complete Short Stories of Ernest Hemingway*. New York: Charles Scribner's Sons/ MacMillan, 1987.

Hillairet, Jacques. *Dictionnaire historiques des rues de Paris*. Paris: Les Editions de Minuit, 1978.

Hobhouse, Janet. *Everybody Who Was Anybody: A Biography of Gertrude Stein*. New York: G. P. Putnam and Sons, 1975.

Huddleston, Sisley. *Paris Salons, Cafés, Studios*. New York: Blue Ribbon, 1928.

Huffington, Arianna Stassinopoulos. *Picasso Creator and Destroyer*. New York: Simon and Schuster, 1988.

Hugh, H. P. "The Two Montmartres." *Paris Magazine,* June 1899.

Hunter, Sam. *Modern French Painting, 1855–1956*. New York: Dell, 1960.

James, Henry. *The Ambassadors*. New York: The New American Library, 1979.

Josephson, Matthew. *Life Among the Surrealists*. New York: Holt, Rinehart and Winston, 1962.

Josephson, Matthew. *Stendhal*. New York: Doubleday, 1946.

Kelder, Diane. *Great Masters of French Impressionism from the National Gallery of Art*. New York: Crown, 1986.

Kert, Bernice. *The Hemingway Women*. New York: W. W. Norton, 1983.

Kluver, Billy. *Kiki's Paris: Artists and Lovers, 1900–1930*. New York: Abrams, 1989.

Kuhn, Irene Corbally. "Paris in the Twenties." *Gourmet,* March 1988.

Laclotte, Michel, Geneviève Lacambre, Anne Distel, and Clair Frèches-Thory. *Painting in the Musée d'Orsay*. Paris: Editions de la Réunion des musées nationaux, 1986.

Lauritzen Peter. "The Palazza Contarini-Décazes." *Architectural Digest,* Dec. 1988.

Lemaitre, Georges. *From Cubism to Surrealism in French Literature*. Cambridge: Harvard University, 1941.

Lewis, R. W. B. *Edith Wharton.* New York: Harper and Row, 1975.

Liebman, Lisa. "Braque Steps Out of the Long Shadow Cast by Picasso." *Smithsonian,* July 1988.

Lipton, Eunice. "The Sadness of Artists." *New York Times,* 17 July 1988.

Lieberman, Alexander. *The Artist in his Studio.* New York: Random House, 1988.

Liebling, A. J. *Between Meals, An Appetite for Paris.* San Francisco: North Point Press, 1986.

Littlewood, Ian. *Paris, a Literary Companion.* London: John Murray, 1987.Maddox, Brenda. *Nora.* Boston: Houghton Mifflin, 1988.

Looking at Paris. Paris: Réalities-Hachette, 1973.

Mathieu, Caroline. "1889. La Tour Eiffel et l'exposition universelle." *Revue de Louvre,* March 1989.

Mathieu, Caroline. *Guide to the Musée d'Orsay.* Paris: Edition de la Réunion des musées nationaux, 1987.

Maugham, W. Somerset. *The Razor's Edge.* Philadelphia: The Blakiston Co., 1945.

McAlmon, Robert, and Kay Boyle. *Being Geniuses Together 1920–1930.* San Francisco: North Point, 1984.

Méikian, Souren. "The First Shimmers of Impressionism." *Réalités,* Paris: Sociétés d'etudes et de publications economeque, Dec. 1969.

Meisler, Stanley. "Soutine: The Power and the Fury of an Eccentric Genius." *Smithsonian,* Nov. 1988.

Mellow, James. *Charmed Circle.* New York: Avon Books, 1982.

Meltzer, Charles H. "Sarah Bernhardt." *Beacon Lights of History.* Edited by George S. Hulbert. New York: Wm. H. Wise and Co., 1924.

Menkes, Suzy. "Dior Signals a Brave New World of Haute Couture." *International Herald Tribune,* 16 May 1989.

Mermillon, Maurius. *Maurice Utrillo.* Paris: Les editions Braun, 1950.

Milbank, Caroline Rennolds. *Couture.* New York: Stewart, Tabori and Chang, 1985.

Milford, Nancy. *Zelda.* New York: Harper and Row, 1970.

Miller, Henry. *Black Spring.* New York: Grove Press, 1963.

Miller, Henry. *Tropic of Cancer.* New York: Grove Press, 1961.

Monnier, Adrienne. *The Very Rich Hours of Adrienne Monnier.* Translated by Richard MacDougall. New York: Charles Scribner's Sons, 1976.

Morel, Dominique. *Maison Renan-Scheffer.* Paris: Les musées de la ville de Paris, 1988.

Morley, Sheridan. *Oscar Wilde.* New York: Holt, Rinehart and Winston, 1976.

Morton, Brian N. *Americans in Paris.* Ann Arbor: The Olivia and Hill Press, 1984.Murger, Henri. *La Bohème.* Salt Lake City: Gibbs M. Smith, 1988.

"The New the Enduring Paris." *National Geographic,* July 1989.

Oberthur, Mariel. *Cafés and Cabarets of Montmartre.* Salt Lake City: Gibbs M. Smith, 1984.

Orwell, George. *Down and Out in Paris and London.* London: Seeker and Warburg, 1949.

Palmer, Alexandra. "Collecting Couture." *Architectural Digest,* Sept. 1989.

Perlès, Alfred. *My Friend, Henry Miller.* New York: Belmont Books, 1962.

Regan, Kate. "Dazzling Remnants of Diaghilev Ballets." *San Francisco Examiner Review,* 18 Dec. 1988.

Renoir, Jean. *Renoir, My Father.* London: Little, Brown, 1962.

Rewald, John. *The History of Impressionism.* New York: The Museum of Modern Art, 1946.

Rhys, Jean. *Quartet.* New York: Vintage Books, 1974.

Richardson, Joanna. *Colette.* New York: Dell, 1985.

Richardson, John. "Degas's Ladies of the Night." *Vanity Fair,* Aug. 1988.

Richardson, John. "Picasso Pentimento." *Vanity Fair,* Dec. 1989.

Rochegude and Clébert. *Promenades*

dans les rues de Paris. Paris: Club des Libraries de France, 1958.

Root, Waverly. *The Paris Edition*. San Francisco: North Point Press, 1987.

Rose, Phyllis. *Jazz Cleopatra, Josephine Baker in Her Time*. New York: Doubleday, 1989.

Rosen, Barbara. "Picasso Sold for $40.7 Million." *San Francisco Chronicle*, 16 Nov. 1989.

Russell, John. "Two Who Made a Revolution." *New York Times*, 17 Sept. 1989.

Sabartés, Jaime. *Picasso: An Intimate Portrait*. New York: Prentice-Hall Inc., 1948.

Saroyan, William. *Here Comes, There Goes, You Know Who*. New York: Simon and Schuster, 1961.

Schwartz, Charles. *Gershwin, His Life and Music*. London: Abelard/Schuman, 1973.

Shattuck, Roger. *The Banquet Years*. New York: Vintage, 1968.

Silver, Kenneth E. *Esprit de Corps*. Princeton: Princeton University Press, 1989.

Skinner, Cornelius Otis. *Madame Sarah*. Boston: Houghton Mifflin, 1966.

Smith, Roberta. "When Japan Captured the French Imagination." *New York Times*, 6 Aug. 1988.

Sokoloff, Alice Hunt. *Hadley: The First Mrs. Hemingway*. New York: Dodd, Mead, 1973.

Stein, Gertrude. *Picasso*. London: B. T. Batsford, 1938.

Stein, Gertrude. "The Autobiography of Alice B. Toklas." *Selected Writings of Gertrude Stein*. Edited by Carl Van Vechten. New York: Random House, 1972.

Stein, Gertrude. "Three Portraits of Painters." *Selected Writings of Gertrude Stein*. Edited by Carl Van Vechten. New York: Random House, 1972

Stein Gertrude. *The World Is Round*. San Francisco: North Point Press, 1988.

Stevenson, R. L. *Inland Voyage and Innocents Abroad*. New York: Wm. H. Wise, 1926.

Stone, Judy. "Vincent: Self Portrait from Letters of Van Gogh." *San Francisco Chronicle*, 10 Aug. 1988.

Stone, Irving. *Dear Theo*. New York: New American Library, 1934.

Stone, Irving. *Depths of Glory*. New York: Doubleday, 1985.

Stone, Irving. *Lust for Life*. New York: Doubleday, 1984.

Sutton, Denys. *Edgar Degas: Life and Work*. New York: Rizzoli, 1986.

Toklas, Alice B. *The Alice B. Toklas Cookbook*. New York: Harper and Row, 1954.

Thomson, Virgil. *Selected Letters of Virgil Thomson*. Edited by Tim Page and Vanessa Weeks Page. New York: Summit, 1988.

Tomkins, Calvin. "Irises." *The New Yorker*, 4 April 1988.

Tomkins, Calvin. *Living Well is the Best Revenge*. New York: Viking Press, 1962.

Vollard, Ambroise. *Renoir, An Intimate Record*. New York: Alfred A. Knopf, 1925.

Wadley, Nicholas, ed. *Renoir A Retrospective*. New York: Park Lane, 1987..

Wagner, Mary T. "Josephine Baker: From Poverty to Paris and Back." *San Francisco Examiner*, 26 Feb. 1989.

Weber, Eugen. "Paris, La Belle Epoque." *National Geographic*, July 1989.

Werner, Alfred. *Utrillo*. New York: Harry N. Abrams, 1953.

Wickes, George. *Americans in Paris*. New York: Doubleday, 1969.

Williams W. C. *The Autobiography of William Carlos Williams*. New York: New Directions, 1948.

Wiser, William. "Paris Revisited." *Paris Magazine*, Paris: Shakespeare and Co., 1984.

Wiser, William. *The Crazy Years, Paris in the Twenties*. New York: G. K. Hall, 1985.

Wurman, Richard. *Paris Access*. New York: Access Press Ltd., 1987.

Zola, Emile. *Nana*. London: Harmondsworth, 1980.

ACKNOWLEDGMENTS

The assistance of Jack Casford, Eva Maas, George Whitman, and Raymond L. Haight is gratefully appreciated.

Many thanks for graciously contributing photographs go to Thomas Gee; Andrew and Duncan McElhone of Harry's New York Bar; Eric Turmel, press representative for Jeanne Lanvin S.A.; and Véronique Perez, press-attaché for Chanel.

Special thanks to Bob Burnip and Tom Ryan who, during a long walk in Paris, encouraged me to write this book.

INDEX